6. Pray for God's help. You *need* God's help in order to understand what you study in the Bible. PSALM 119:18 would be an appropriate v   ~rayer.

7. *Class t*  *group study will find some helpf*

how to

take the self-check tests

Each lesson is concluded with a test designed to help you evaluate what you have learned.

1. Review the lesson carefully in the light of the self-check test questions.

2. If there are any questions in the self-check test you cannot answer, perhaps you have written into your lesson the wrong answer from your Bible. Go over your work carefully to make sure you have filled in the blanks correctly.

3. When you think you are ready to take the self-check test, do so without looking up the answers.

4. Check your answers to the self-check test carefully with the answer key given on page 64.

5. If you have any questions wrong, your answer key will tell you where to find the correct answer in your lesson. Go back and locate the right answers. Learn by your mistakes!

apply

what you have learned

to your own life

In this connection, read carefully JAMES 1:22-25. It is only as you apply your lessons to your own life that you will really grow in grace and increase in the knowledge of God.

The Son of God— Better than Prophets and Angels

1:1-14

"... so much better" (1:4)

No one knows who wrote Hebrews. Many arguments have been advanced to try to prove that Paul wrote it; many other arguments, that Paul did not write it. None is conclusive. The heading we now find in our Bibles, *The Epistle of Paul the Apostle to the Hebrews,* was almost certainly not on the autograph. However, the contents of the epistle are so evidently inspired by God that it makes little difference who the human author was. The book was written to Hebrew Christians, probably about A.D. 66, shortly before the destruction of Jerusalem (A.D. 70), for the Temple was still standing and the priests were still ministering there (10:11).

The key words are "faith" and "better." "Faith" occurs thirty-two times; "better," thirteen times. Christ is *better* than all others, and He is appropriated by *faith.* In addition, the exhortation "let us," occurring thirteen times, is the key phrase. Hence, throughout the epistle we should expect an emphasis on the superiority of Jesus Christ, on our need for complete faith in Him, and on exhortations for us to obey Him in certain attitudes and deeds.

The Son of God—better than prophets (1:1-3)

1. What truth does the writer stress in the first two verses to show the unity between the Old and the New Testaments?

1:1, 2 _____

_____

In the Greek, the words "at sundry times" mean "in many parts." An English equivalent would be "fragmentarily." It had not been God's method to reveal much at a time, but to lift the veil fold by fold as humanity was able to receive it. The truth had been revealed "in divers manners"—by dreams, visions and direct inspiration.

2. But who now brings the full and final revelation of truth?

1:2 _____

3. Why is this One in a position to give the ultimate revelation?

1:2 _____

_____

4. Why must the Lord Jesus Christ be the Heir of all things?

1:2 (last clause); JOHN 1:3 _____

_____

5. What brought the Creator and Upholder of all things down to this small earth?

1:3 _____

6. What two words indicate the lonely and exclusive character of Christ's redemptive work?

1:3 _____

3

7. Why could no one else in all the universe offer such a sacrifice for the sins of mankind?

9:12; I JOHN 1:7 _____

_____

8. What expressions in verse 3 indicate the absolute deity of Jesus Christ?

1:3 "Being _____,

and _____,

and upholding _____

_____."

Going back before history, the writer sees Christ as the very outshining of the glory of the Godhead. Without Him God would be darkness to us by the very excess of His brightness. The light of the sun is so exceedingly bright that it is unbearable, but put a pan of water down and you can see its image reflected. Cast the eye of faith upon Jesus and you have a bearable reflex of the glory of God. The words rendered "express image" really mean "a stamp" or an impression left by a stamp or engraving instrument. Deity was stamped upon Him and He conveys that impression to men. It is interesting to know that the word "character" comes from "an engraving instrument" or "marks cut by such an instrument," later coming to mean "marks cut in personality." Christ *is* the Character of God.

The Son of God—better than angels (1:4-14)

In these verses, there are six quotations from the Old Testament which demonstrate the infinite superiority of this "better" One.

4

9. Because Jesus is the exalted, incarnate Son of God, what does He possess that sets Him above the angels of God?

1:4 _____.

10. What else does He possess—something He has "obtained"—that is "more excellent"?

8:6 _____

11. What does Paul say about His name?

PHILIPPIANS 2:9 _____

The words concerning the Son, quoted in HEBREWS 1:5a, were fulfilled "in that he [God] raised up Jesus" (ACTS 13:32, 33, American Standard Version[1]).

12. What fact fully demonstrated that Jesus is "the Son of God with power"?

ROMANS 1:4 _____

13. What did the Son say to God at His incarnation?

10:7; 10:5-7 _____

_____

14. What will God say to all the angels when He "again bringeth in the firstborn into the world" (1:6, A.S.V.)[2]?

1:6 _____

15. Who is the Son—irrefutable proof that He is superior to angels?

1:8 _____

[1]In the pages that follow, quotations from this version, published in 1901, are indicated by the abbreviation, A.S.V.

[2]The quotation in HEBREWS 1:6 is from DEUTERONOMY 32:43, Septuagint Version, the Greek translation of the Old Testament used by Christ and His apostles. This verse is not in the King James Version.

16. What two things is Christ said to have created?

1:10; Colossians 1:16 _____

17. Regardless of what happens to earth and "the heavens," what is certain about the Son?

1:10-12 _____

_____

18. What did Jesus say about Himself?

Revelation 1:17 _____

19. What did Jesus say as to His own eternal existence?

John 8:58 _____

20. What is the function of angels?

1:14 _____

21. How many angelic creatures are there?

12:22 _____

22. Through whom, as His representatives, does Stephen say God gave the law to Israel?

Acts 7:53 _____

23. Through whom does Paul say the law was given into the hand of a mediator (Moses)?

Galatians 3:19 _____

The first chapter of Hebrews makes it clear that the Son of God is infinitely superior to the prophets, through whom the Old Testament was given, and to the angels, through whom the law was given to Moses.

The Son of Man— Better than Angels

2:1-18

> "We see Jesus . . . a merciful and faithful high priest." (2:9, 17)

HEBREWS 2 falls logically into two distinct parts: a parenthesis (verses 1-4); and a continuation of Christ's superiority to angels —as Son of Man (verses 5-18).

"How shall we escape if we neglect . . .?" (2:1-4)

The writer thinks continually of the peril facing a Hebrew who has professed to receive Jesus as the Messiah yet lapses into Judaism in the face of the overwhelming evidence that had been given concerning the deity of the Lord Jesus Christ.

The peril these Hebrews faced in not giving careful heed to what they had heard is expressed in these words: ". . . lest haply we drift away from them" (2:1, A.S.V.).

1. Why was their danger so much greater if they neglected "so great salvation" than the danger of those who transgressed the law?

2:2, 3 Because the law was "spoken by _____,"

but this "great salvation" was originally spoken by "_____

_____."

2. What increases the condemnation of those who neglect this "great salvation"?

2:3 (last clause) _____

3. What proof was given by God "at the first" to confirm the revelation ministered by Christ and by those who had heard Him?

2:4 _____

_____

4. What phrase, apart from the expression "at the first," suggests that these signs and wonders might not continue to be given indefinitely?

2:4 (final words) _____

Read carefully DEUTERONOMY 4:9-12, noting such phrases as these: "lest thou forget," "lest they depart from thy heart." Then answer this question with "Yes" or "No":

5. Did the wonders that confirmed the message of Sinai continue in the same measure throughout the period of the law? _____

You will find that there are certain great miracle zones in the Bible, related to great crises or to the opening of a new dispensation or revelation. The signs and wonders taper off, but the truth and experience remain.

6. How does Christ describe the peril from which "so great salvation" was designed to provide an escape?

MATTHEW 23:33 _____

7. To what result can "neglect" lead as surely as outright rejection?

JOHN 3:18 _____

The Son of Man—better than angels (2:5-18)

Read PSALMS 8:4-6; 22:22; ISAIAH 8:17, 18. Then find the verses in HEBREWS 2 in which these four passages are quoted to show that the perfect humanity of the Son of Man was foretold in the Old Testament.

8. To whom has God subjected the world [Greek, "the inhabited earth," A.S.V., margin] to come?

2:6-8 _____

9. What is His human name?

2:9 _____

"God originally gave dominion over all the earth to man. . . . Man forfeited this honor when he sinned. . . . By becoming Man, and dying for the sins of man, Christ has regained for man the dominion he had lost."—William MacDonald.

10. Why was He made "a little lower than the angels"?

2:9 _____

11. What dignity has now been accorded Him?

2:9 _____

12. What did God's grace require that He should do first?

2:9 _____

13. How far-reaching was the purpose of Christ's death?

a. HEBREWS 2:9 (last phrase) _____

b. I TIMOTHY 2:6 _____

14. What title is here given to Christ?

2:10 _____

The words "all are of one" (2:11) mean that "all are of one humanity, flesh and blood; or all are of one Father."—William MacDonald. The Son of Man thus identifies Himself with His "brethren"!

9

15. For what specific purpose did Christ take human form and come among men?

2:14 _____ _____

_____

"Destroy" here means, not "annihilate," but "bring to naught."

16. What happens to Satan's grip on a person when that person is born again?

COLOSSIANS 1:13 _____

17. From what dread is a real believer delivered?

2:15 _____

18. Through whom does God give the victory over sin and death?

I CORINTHIANS 15:54-57 _____

19. Why did the Lord desire to take human form?

2:17 _____

_____

20. What two qualities does Christ possess as our perfect High Priest?

2:17 _____

21. Why can no temptation or trial come to us that He does not perfectly understand?

2:18 _____

Alexander Maclaren says: "Comfort drops but coldly from lips that have never uttered a sigh or a groan, and for our poor human hearts it is not enough to have a God far off in heaven. We need a Saviour who can be touched with the feeling of our infirmity, ere we can come boldly to the throne of grace."

check-up time No. 1

You have just studied some important truths in Hebrews 1 and 2. Review your study by rereading the questions and your written answers. If you are not sure about an answer, reread the Scripture text given to check it. Then take the following test to see how well you understand and remember important truths you have studied.

In the right-hand margin write "True" or "False" after each of the following statements.

1. The full and final revelation of God is seen in the holy angels. _____

2. The two words in HEBREWS 1:3 that suggest the lonely character of Christ's redemptive work are "by himself." _____

3. It is Jesus' more excellent name that sets Him above the angels. _____

4. Angels are mere ministers, but the Son is God. _____

5. Stephen says the law was given to Israel by Moses. _____

6. It is impossible for the Christian to escape the fear of death. _____

7. The phrase, "according to his own will," suggests that miracles might not continue indefinitely. _____

8. Neglect, as well as rejection, can lead to condemnation. _____

9. Jesus was made a little lower than the angels (2:9) for the suffering of temptation. _____

10. Christ became Man to destroy the devil. _____

Turn to page 64 and check your answers.

Christ—
Better than Moses

3:1-19

_____

> "Moses . . . was faithful . . . as a servant . . . but
> Christ as a son." (3:5, 6)

In chapters 3–7 Christ is shown to be superior to both Moses and Aaron, and to all for which they stood. The Jews regarded the dispensation of law as supreme because (a) it was ministered by angels; (b) it was in the hands of a mediator of exalted character, Moses; (c) its principal representative, the high priest, held superior authority. The writer now proceeds to compare Christ with the two great officials of the old dispensation: the mediator and the high priest.

Christ—"worthy of more glory than Moses" (3:1-6)

1. To whom does the writer here appeal?

3:1; I Thessalonians 5:27 _____

2. To what two phases of the work of Christ does the writer call attention?

3:1 _____

3. For what purpose was Christ an "Apostle" ("Sent One")?

a. GALATIANS 4:4, 5 _____

b. I JOHN 4:10 _____

4. What title was used of the coming Messiah at the end of the Old Testament?

MALACHI 3:1 _____

As Apostle (or Prophet), Jesus pleads the cause of God with us. As High Priest, He pleads the believer's cause with the Father. Combining the two, He is our Mediator.

5. What special characteristic did Moses possess?

3:2; NUMBERS 12:7 _____

6. While fully recognizing the dignity of Moses, what does the Holy Spirit say about the worth of Christ?

3:3a _____

7. Why is Christ so superior to Moses?

3:3b _____

8. What is to be accorded to Christ?

COLOSSIANS 1:18 _____

In several ways Moses was a type of Christ. As infants, they were both threatened by cruel rulers, yet marvelously sheltered. Both were prophets. Moses was a mediator between God and Israel, but Jesus—Prophet, Priest and King—is the one and final Mediator between God and man. From Mount Sinai Moses brought the law on tables of stone; Jesus, by His Spirit, writes them in the hearts of men.

9. What was Moses' position in the house of God's building?

3:4, 5 _____

10. What is Christ's position "over his [God's] house" (A.S.V.)?

3:6 _____

11. How does the writer suggest that the things of Moses were typical and prophetic?

3:5 _____

_____

12. What did God reveal to Moses in this connection?

DEUTERONOMY 18:15-19 _____

_____

13. Of whom, in particular, did Moses and others prophesy?

LUKE 24:27, 44 _____

14. What did Jesus say about Moses?

JOHN 5:46 _____

The writer of Hebrews in no sense lowers the dignity of Moses. He was faithful to his divine appointment, but he was only a part of the great household of God. Jesus is faithful as the Son and Heir over the house, of which God Himself is the Builder. "Over his own house" (3:6) should be "over his [God's] house." The dispensation of Moses was preparatory, typical, temporary.

15. Who is now the one Mediator between God and men?

I TIMOTHY 2:5 _____

16. How does the writer of Hebrews describe the Christian?

3:6 _____

17. In what way are true believers referred to in connection with God's building?

a. By Paul? EPHESIANS 2:19-22 _____

b. By Peter? I PETER 2:5 _____

"Lively" should be "living" here.

Israel's unbelief—a warning "today" (3:7-19)

HEBREWS 3:7-19 contains a parenthetical exhortation (based on PSALM 95:7-11) to believe God, and not forfeit the blessings which come through faith as had many of the Israelites of old.

18. What had Israel done to provoke God in the wilderness?

3:8 _____

Verse 9 might be paraphrased: "Your fathers tried my patience, tested my forbearance and witnessed my works for forty years." Yet they doubted the *power* of God (NUMBERS 13:27, 28, 33); doubted the *love* of God (NUMBERS 14:1-5); doubted the *word* of God (NUMBERS 14:11).

19. What similar sin of unbelief were the Jews in peril of committing at this time?

2:3, 4 _____

20. What lesson do we today need to learn from the Israelites who, in the face of a glorious revelation from God, murmured and rebelled against Him?

I CORINTHIANS 10:9-12 _____

21. What word is emphasized, by repetition, in this passage?

3:7, 13, 15 _____

15

22. Why is it so urgent that we trust Christ and turn our lives over to Him?

JAMES 4:14 _____

23. To what greater depth than the mind may the root of skepticism sometimes go?

3:12 _____

The foregoing does not mean that one should not think things through. If he has honest doubts, he should go on through them to faith.

24. What is it that causes doubts to become full unbelief?

JOHN 3:19, 20 _____

25. What is the trouble with the human heart?

JEREMIAH 17: 9 _____

26. Because of this, what should Christians do?

3:13 _____

27. If we are really "partakers of Christ," what will we do?

3:14 _____

The writer of Hebrews was fearful lest some who professed to acknowledge Jesus as their Messiah had not really been born again. Otherwise, they would not have been turning back to Judaism—much as many Israelites had hankered after Egypt and failed to enter Canaan (3:16-18).

28. What caused many Israelites to perish in the wilderness?

3:19 _____

29. Why can the mere hearing and approving of gospel sermons save no one?

4:2 _____

Christ—
Better than Joshua

4:1—16

> "For if Joshua had given them rest. . . . There remaineth therefore a sabbath rest for the people of God." (4:8, 9 A.S.V.)

In chapter 4 Christ is shown to be superior to Joshua as well as to Moses. (Note that "Jesus," verse 8, Authorized Version, is the Greek form of "Joshua.")

Christ can lead us into God's rest (4:1-11)

1. What four exhortations in this chapter begin with "Let us"?

a. Verse 1 _____ _____

b. Verse 11 _____

c. Verse 14 _____

d. Verse 16 _____

2. The writer was concerned lest his readers fail to do what?

4:1 _____

3. What did he want them to possess, lest the gospel they had heard should be of no profit to them?

4:2 _____

4. What is true of all who put their trust in the Lord?

PSALM 2:12 _____

5. What is true of those who have a genuine "fear of God" in their hearts?

JEREMIAH 32:40 _____

A genuine "fear of God" denotes a deep reverence for God springing from real faith in God.

6. What had been the trouble with the Israelites in the wilderness who had failed to enter Canaan?

4:2; 3:19 _____

7. What was Isaiah's searching question or complaint against his people?

ISAIAH 53:1 _____

8. If the gospel is to profit us and actually give us rest, with what must it be mixed?

4:2 _____

9. What do those who have really believed the gospel do?

4:3 _____

10. What does Paul call this rest?

ROMANS 5:1 _____

"If they shall enter" (verses 3 and 5) is translated, "They shall not enter" (A.S.V.). God's rest was waiting for His people of old; but because of their unbelief, He decreed that they should not enter into it. (See ISAIAH 28:12.)

11. What was required to obtain rest under the law?

JEREMIAH 6:16 _____

18

12. What is required now, under grace?

MATTHEW 11:28 _____

13. By what means have we who once were "far off" been "made nigh," and given peace or rest?

EPHESIANS 2:13, 14 _____

14. Who failed to give Israel rest in the long ago?

4:8 (A.S.V.) _____

15. What are we to labor, or "give diligence" (A.S.V.), to do?

4:11 _____

16. By what means does Paul say it is impossible to enter into God's rest, that is, be saved?

EPHESIANS 2:8, 9_____

The Word of God exposes unbelief (4:12, 13)

17. What facts make it a perilous thing to trifle with the Word of God?

4:12 _____

_____

18. What does Paul call the Word of God?

EPHESIANS 6:17 _____

19. To what extent is the Word of God able to expose a person completely?

4:12 _____

_____

19

20. As one reads the Word of God, what is he apt to discover?

PSALM 139:1-4 _____

_____

21. Into what greater depths than our minds does the Word of God probe?

4:12 (last clause) _____

22. Can we hide anything from God?

4:13 _____

"We have a great high priest" (4:14-16)

Verses 14-16 introduce the subject of chapters 5–7: "Christ— better than the Aaronic priesthood."

23. What have we already learned about Christ as our High Priest?

a. 2:17 _____

b. 3:1 _____

24. Since all true believers have such a great High Priest, what are they urged to do?

4:14 _____

25. What is our great High Priest later called with reference to us who believe?

6:20 _____

26. What fact should encourage us to put our confidence in this great High Priest?

4:15 _____

27. What fact has made the Lord Jesus able to feel our infirmities?

JOHN 1:14 _____

28. What distinguishes Him sharply from the high priests of the Aaronic order?

4:15 (last phrase) _____

29. To what extent is He able to sympathize with us in all our burdens, even though He was and is without sin?

ISAIAH 53:4 _____

The fact that the risen Christ is a Man at the right hand of God should greatly encourage and strengthen every believer. How very much it means to us to have in heaven a great High Priest who is able to feel everything that distresses each one of His own!

check-up time No. 2

You have now studied some important truths in Hebrews 3 and 4. Review your study by reading the questions and your written answers. If you are uncertain about an answer, reread the Scripture reference to check your answer. Then take the following test to see how well you understand and remember important truths you have studied.

In the right-hand margin write "True" or "False" after each of the following statements.

1. In HEBREWS 3:1 Christ is referred to as Apostle and High Priest.   _____

2. In MALACHI 3:1 the coming Messiah is referred to as God's Lamb.   _____

3. In JOHN 5:46 Jesus says of Moses, "Among them that are born of women there hath not risen a greater . . . ."   _____

4. In HEBREWS 3:6 Christ is referred to as a Son over His (God's) house.   _____

5. Hearing a gospel message and approving of it often saves a soul.   _____

6. One of the four exhortations in HEBREWS 4 is "Let us love."   _____

7. The ancient Israelites did not enter into rest because the gospel they heard was not mixed with fear.   _____

8. Those who really believe the gospel enter into God's rest.   _____

9. The means whereby believers have been given rest is the sinlessness of Christ.   _____

10. No one can hide anything from God.   _____

Turn to page 64 and check your answers.

Christ— Better than Aaron

5:1-14

"A priest forever after the order of Melchisedec" (5:6)

The theme developed in chapters 5–7 may be stated like this: Christ is superior to Aaron and the entire Aaronic or Levitical priesthood. Bear in mind that the Hebrews were reared in an atmosphere of smoking altars, and you can understand how welcome this unfolding of the priesthood of the Lord Jesus was to the distracted minds of those Hebrews who had become Christions. At last, a High Priest forever, after the order of Melchisedec, doing away with the Levitical priesthood! Before Israel had been redeemed from Egypt, sacrifices and offerings were brought by the heads of families—a Passover lamb is every household. Later when, by the Mosaic Law, the people were made more conscious of sin and of the holiness of God, a priesthood was appointed, typical of the true mediation that was eventually to be found in their Messiah.

The qualifications and duties of a high priest fulfilled in Christ (5:1-10)

1. What two things was every Aaronic high priest expected to do?

5:1 _____

2. Being "compassed with infirmity" himself, what attitude was he to have toward others?

5:2 _____

3. Because of his own sinfulness, what did the Aaronic priest have to do?

5:3 _____

4. Although He was always without sin, what two qualities does Jesus possess as our High Priest?

2:17 _____

5. In spite of His absolute sinlessness, what capacity has He?

4:15 _____

While the Aaronic priests could sympathize with their people as fellow sinners, Christ has perfect insight into hearts. He felt all the force of satanic pressu without yielding and went to the heart of the sin question. He knows its origin and all the circumstances leading up to it. While we might expect the perfect Man to be more severe as Judge, He is the more merciful High Priest. He was more compassionate with the harlot and drunkard who had little light than with the selfish, respectable, hypocritical religionist.

6. In what respect did Christ resemble the Aaronic high priests?

5:4-6 _____

7. How does God refer to Christ in Psalm 2:6?

_____

8. How does God address Christ in Psalm 110:4?

_____

9. What two offices did Melchisedec fill that make him a particularly appropriate type of Christ?

7:1; GENESIS 14:18 _____

10. Through what trying experience did Jesus pass that enables Him to sympathize with us in our deepest sorrows?

5:7; LUKE 22:41-44 _____

_____

11. When had angelic help been given Him before?

MATTHEW 4:11 _____

12. Who was particularly eager to crush Jesus in some way that would defeat God's purposes for Him as Redeemer and Priest?

LUKE 4:3-13 _____

13. If Jesus had been spared the death of the cross, what would have become of our salvation?

3:14-16; HEBREWS 9:22 _____

_____

14. How was Christ's prayer to be saved out of death (5:7) answered? (The Greek indicates "out of death" rather than "from death.")

PSALM 16:8-11; ACTS 2:25-31 _____

_____

15. What was the purpose of this terrible testing in Gethsemane?

5:8, 9 _____

_____

To be "made perfect" means to be "made complete" not "made sinless or flawless." Thus our Lord was adequately fitted for His work as High Priest. Thank God that we have a Redeemer and

High Priest, "taken from among men," who has felt so keenly the struggle against the sorrows of this life and the powers of darkness!

Spiritual immaturity rebuked (5:11-14)

Now scan quickly HEBREWS 5:11—6:20 and you will see that this portion is a long parenthesis. The central theme of Christ's priesthood is not mentioned between 5:10 and 6:19. The writer realized that those addressed were not ready for the deep truths of Christ's priesthood; hence this rebuke, warning, comfort and exhortation.

16. What was wrong with those to whom this epistle was written? (Is this true of many of us today?)

5:11 _____

17. How can any Christian know these things which God so desires to impart?

I CORINTHIANS 2:9-12 _____

18. What diet do some Christians need because of their immaturity?

5:12 _____

19. If one is spiritually mature, what diet can he enjoy?

5:12-14 _____

20. What is often the real reason Christians cannot digest the meat of the Word?

I CORINTHIANS 3:1-3 _____

21. Can you say what Job and the psalmist said about God's words?

JOB 23:12; PSALM 119:103 _____

Christ—
Our Forerunner

6:1-20

_____

". . . whither the forerunner is for us entered, even Jesus" (6:20)

No nation was ever in greater peril from apostasy and unbelief than the Jews who lived in the days just following the resurrection of our Lord and the outpouring of the Holy Spirit at Pentecost. The writer of this epistle seeks to arouse the Hebrews to sense this peril by a profound exposition of the glory of the exalted Christ, their great High Priest.

Now, in chapter 6, having rebuked them for being "dull of hearing" such wonderful truth (5:11-14), he exhorts them to grow up as Christians and to beware apostasy.

"Let us go on" to Christian maturity (6:1-3)

1. Instead of continuing to lay and re-lay the foundations, what are those addressed urged to do?

6:1 _____

"Perfection" here is "full growth" or "maturity."

The six items of doctrine mentioned in verses 1 and 2 seem to be principles concerning the Messiah as taught in the Old Testament. The writer says it is pointless to continue going over these teachings again and again instead of going on to the characteristic doctrines of Christianity.

27

The danger of apostasy (6:4-8)

These verses must be viewed in connection with the special circumstances of the Jews of that time. The gospel had been preached to them in full; they had seen the gifts and powers of the Holy Spirit manifested in a marvelous way. Some had received Christ as their Saviour. Others had *seemed* to receive Him and to enter into the sphere of new covenant manifestation. Now what if any of them should lapse into the legalism of Judaism? That would be a situation full of the gravest peril.

2. What strong word shows that the statements of verses 4-6 *cannot* apply to a true child of God who has fallen by the way, or backslidden?

6:4 (fourth word) _____

3. What does Scripture teach about the possibility of restoration for the backslider?

PSALM 23:3; HOSEA 14:4; I JOHN 1:9 _____

_____

4. Is a person necessarily born again because he has been "enlightened" or instructed concerning the gospel?

6:4; JOHN 1:9-11 _____

5. Is one necessarily born again because he has "tasted of the heavenly gift"?

6:4 _____

See MATTHEW 27:34 where the same Greek word is used for "tasted" as in HEBREWS 6:4, 5.

6. Is one necessarily born again because he has been made a "partaker" of the convicting work of the Holy Spirit?

6:4; JOHN 16:7-9 _____

7. Is one necessarily born again because he has "tasted" the good Word of God, and likes to hear sermons based on the Bible?

6:5; Ezekiel 33:31, 32 _____

8. Is one necessarily born again because he has "tasted" the powers of the age to come, or sampled the good things of the age of grace—even "believing" perhaps in his mind but not in his heart, and witnessing the miracle of the new birth in others?

6:5; Acts 8:12-23 _____

9. If a Hebrew, with a full knowledge of the highest evidence that heaven could give concerning the deity of Christ, should turn back and again ally himself with those who had rejected Christ as a blasphemer, he would be guilty of what terrible sin?

6:6 _____

_____ and _____ _____

10. What statement shows that this stern warning was not written *to* such Hebrews, but *about* such?

6:9 _____

The writer had not the slightest doubt of the salvation of those who had truly received Jesus as their Messiah. One translation of verse 9 reads as follows: "Though I use the language of such stern warning, I am sure that this is not your condition." He was using strong words to warn any who might be triflers.

Verses 4-6 may doubtless be applied today to all who wilfully and finally reject the Saviour after they have learned the truth about Him and His salvation.

Note the illustration from nature in verses 7 and 8, and how it emphasizes the warning of verses 4-6.

Assurance of salvation for the believer in Christ (6:9-20)

11. What kind of fruit will the Holy Spirit produce in a real Christian?

EPHESIANS 5:9 _____

12. What proved to the writer of Hebrews that those addressed were truly Christian believers?

6:10 _____

_____

Read carefully GENESIS 22:15-18 and HEBREWS 6:13-18. Abraham had waited more than twenty-five years for the fulfillment of God's promise of a son, Isaac. (See GENESIS 11:31–12:4; 21: 5.)

13. In the light of GENESIS 22:18; MATTHEW 1:1; and GALATIANS 3:8, what did God's promise also include?

_____

14. How did God confirm His promise to Abraham?

6:17 _____

God's promise, confirmed by His oath—"two immutable things" (6:18)—what assurance of salvation for the believer in Christ!

15. Where is the believer's hope—the anchor of the soul—grounded?

6:19, 20 _____

Aaron was a *representative* of his people when he entered the Holy of Holies on the Day of Atonement. Our great High Priest is our *Forerunner* into heaven itself (6:20). Thus He guarantees that all of His redeemed children will follow Him there.

check-up time No. 3

You have now studied some important truths in Hebrews 5 and 6. Review these by rereading the questions and your written answers. If you are uncertain about an answer, reread the Scripture text given to check the answer. Then take the following test to see how well you have understood and remembered the important truths you have studied.

In the right-hand margin write "True" or "False" after each of the following statements.

1. It was the duty of every Aaronic high priest to offer gifts and sacrifices for sins. _____

2. The Aaronic priest offered no sacrifice for himself. _____

3. Because of His sinlessness, Jesus has difficulty in feeling our infirmities. _____

4. Christ is a Priest forever after the order of Aaron. _____

5. Jesus' prayer to be saved out of death was answered. _____

6. The writer urges the Hebrew Christians to "go on to perfection." _____

7. The writer of Hebrews says it is impossible to renew certain people to repentance. _____

8. Aaron was the believer's forerunner within the veil. _____

9. If a person has "tasted" the good Word of God, he is certain to be born again. _____

10. The writer of Hebrews is addressing real believers in Christ. _____

Turn to page 64 and check your answers.

Christ— a Priest Forever

7:1-28

"... able also to save ... to the uttermost" (7:25)

The writer continues his explanation regarding the imperfect, temporary and typical nature of the Levitical system, and its replacement by the enduring priesthood of Christ—"a priest forever after the order of Melchisedec."

1. Regarding Israel's Messiah, what had been said in the Old Testament

a. as to His Person?

PSALM 2:7; HEBREWS 5:5 _____

b. as to His work?

PSALM 110:4; HEBREWS 5:6 _____

2. Where does He exercise His high priestly work?

6:19, 20 _____

Melchisedec—a type of Christ (7:1-3)

3. What unusual combination of offices do we find in Melchisedec?

7:1; GENESIS 14:18 _____

Apart from Melchisedec, there is no other priestly figure mentioned in the Bible prior to the Aaronic priesthood.

4. Is this king-priest mentioned in any genealogy in the Bible?

7:3 _____

"Without descent" means "without genealogy" (A.S.V.). We cannot trace Melchisedec's ancestry or descent, his birth or death. He "abideth a priest continually" (7:3) indicates that there is no *record* of the ending of his priesthood. Thus he is an excellent type of Christ, the eternal Son and Priest.

5. What is the meaning of the name "Melchisedec"?

7:2 _____

6. What is the meaning of the word "Salem"?

7:2 _____

7. Since the priesthood which descended from Abraham (7:5) received tithes from the people, what is remarkable about what Abraham did?

7:2 _____

Melchisedec's priesthood—superior to Aaron's (7:4-10)

8. What does Abraham's giving a tithe to Melchisedec prove?

7:4 _____

9. Would Abraham, who had God's promises, have received a blessing from one whose station was lower than his own?

7:6, 7 _____

10. Would Christ, of the order of Melchisedec, receive a blessing from the Aaronic priesthood?

7:7 _____

Christ's perfect priesthood—superior to Aaron's (7:11-28)

11. What is implied as to the Aaronic priesthood in the fact that the Old Testament foretells the coming of another and eternal order of priesthood?

7:11, 12 _____

12. Was Jesus of Levi, the tribe which furnished all the Levitical priests of Israel?

7:13, 14 _____

13. While every Aaronic priest died and was replaced (7:23), what is true of God's final Priest?

7:16 _____

14. What kind of priesthood do believers have now?

7:24 _____

15. For what two reasons was the Mosaic order regarding the Aaronic priesthood to be set aside?

7:18 _____

16. What blessing does Christ provide which the law could not bestow?

7:19 _____

17. In the establishment of Christ's priesthood, what distinguishes it as superior to that of Aaron?

7:20-22 _____

18. Since, on God's oath, the priesthood of Jesus Christ can never give way to another, what does this mean to the believer?

7:25 _____

Jesus is a perfect Mediator because He is able to give security to both parties to the covenant. By His death He has met the Father's requirements as to the penalty of our sins. By His life at the throne, He meets all our requirements.

19. Since His priesthood is eternal, of what should the believer be absolutely confident?

Philippians 1:6 _____

20. In addition to Christ's past work on the cross, what present work does He do as Priest for the believer?

7:25; Romans 8:34 _____

"To the uttermost" here refers to the end of time and throughout eternity, "seeing he ever liveth."

21. What qualities make the Lord Jesus Christ a suitable High Priest for us?

7:26 _____

_____

22. Why is there now no need for a human priesthood, like the Aaronic?

7:28 _____

What joy that we have a living Lord interceding for us! Throughout eternity our security will rest in the fact that *He ever liveth!*

Christ—the Mediator of a Better Covenant

8:1-13

_____

"Now hath he obtained a more excellent ministry" (8:6)

A new section begins with chapter 8 and continues through 10:18: "The Superiority of the New Covenant over the Old."

Christ—"a minister . . . of the true tabernacle" (8:1-5)

1. What is the most important point made so far in the epistle?

8:1 _____

2. What is significant about Christ's being seated at the right hand of God as contrasted with 10:11?

8:1; 10:12 _____

_____

3. What word is used to indicate Christ's present work as Priest?

8:2 _____

"Minister" here means "servant" or "one active on behalf of another."

4. How do we know that the Old Testament tabernacle was basically symbolic?

8:2; 9:11 _____

_____

5. What was one of the chief ministries of an Aaronic high priest?

8:3 _____

6. What did our Lord Jesus Christ have to offer?

EPHESIANS 5:2 _____

7. What shows that Christ's priestly ministry is heavenly, not earthly?

8:4 _____

8. Of what were the offerings of the Aaronic priests a shadow and example?

8:5 _____

"A more excellent ministry . . . a better covenant" (8:6-13)

9. Christ has now obtained a more excellent ministry (8:6) than that of whom?

8:4 _____

10. Christ is now the Mediator of a better covenant (8:6) than what former covenant?

8:4, 7 _____

11. The better covenant is established upon what better things?

8:6 _____

12. Why should the Hebrews have realized that the covenant of the law was not perfect?

8:7, 8 _____

This new covenant, foretold in JEREMIAH 31:31-34, embraces much more than the present dispensation of grace. It includes the consummation, Israel's restoration to the land of Palestine and the blessings of the kingdom age. Nevertheless, its spiritual application began with the exaltation of Israel's Messiah as High Priest forever. (See I CORINTHIANS 11:25, 26, where "new testament," A.V., is "new covenant," A.S.V.)

13. When was the first covenant established?

8:9 _____

14. What attitude of Israel toward the old covenant caused God to turn from them?

8:9; compare EXODUS 19:5, 6 _____

15. In contrast to the "if ye will" of the old covenant (EXODUS 19:5), what does God promise under the new?

8:10 _____

_____

16. When men come under the new covenant through the new birth, by faith in Christ as Saviour, what does God make them to become?

8:10 (last clause) _____

17. What, according to Paul, is the heart of Christian living?

GALATIANS 2:20a _____

18. To whom, besides Jews, does Paul apply this new covenant?

ROMANS 9:23, 24 _____

19. When the new covenant is fully established (perhaps in the millennium), what will be its scope?

8:11 _____

20. How certain is it that no persecution or tribulation will ever wipe out Israel?

JEREMIAH 31:33-36 _____

_____

21. What wonderful truth applies to *all* who come to God through the Christ (or Messiah) of Israel?

8:12; ACTS 13:38, 39 _____

22. The term "new covenant" indicates what fact about the "old covenant"?

8:13 _____

You have just completed the study of some important truths in Hebrews 7 and 8. Review these by rereading the questions and your written answers. If you are not sure of an answer, reread the Scripture text given and check your answer. Then take the following test to see how well you have understood and remembered the important truths you have studied.

In the right-hand margin write "True" or "False" after each of the following statements.

1. In PSALM 110 Messiah is referred to prophetically as the Prince of Peace. _____

2. Melchisedec was both king and priest. _____

3. Abraham received tithes from Melchisedec. _____

4. Abraham blessed Melchisedec. _____

5. Jesus was made a Priest with an oath. _____

6. As a Priest, Christ stands at the right hand of God. _____

7. The Lord Jesus Christ offered Himself. _____

8. Christ is now the Mediator of a better covenant than that of the law. _____

9. Under the new covenant, God promises, "I will." _____

10. It is probable, but not certain, that Israel will never be wiped out. _____

Turn to page 64 and check your answers.

Christ— the Redeemer

9:1-28

> "By his own blood he . . . obtained eternal redemption." (9:12)

In chapter 9, the old and the new are laid side by side for comparison. Here we see that the Levitical order was given only to Israel for a certain period of their history and that, even for Israel, the shadows had now vanished and the True Light had come. First we see the symbolical character of everything in connection with the old ritual.

The Jewish tabernacle—symbolic of the true tabernacle (9:1-5)

1. What was the chief article of furniture in "the holiest of all," also called the Holy of Holies?

9:3, 4 _____

2. What was the lid of the ark called?

9:5; Exodus 25:21 _____

3. Who is now the believer's mercy seat?

Romans 3:24, 25 _____

The Greek word translated "propitiation" and "mercy seat" means "place of propitiation," where God is satisfied regarding sin. The writer now proceeds to show that Christ, through His shed blood, has made an actual purification of sins.

"The way into the holiest" opened once for all! (9:6-14)

4. What was the one thing the high priest *had* to have when, once a year, he entered into the Holiest of all?

9:7 _____

5. What was it that symbolically opened the way into the Holiest of all? (The veil hung between the Holy Place and the Holy of Holies.)

MATTHEW 27:50, 51 _____

6. What actually opened the way into the Holiest of all in heaven?

10:19, 20 _____

7. What were all the animal sacrifices of the Old Testament unable to do?

9:9 _____

8. The ritual of the law was to be performed until who should come?

9:10, 11; GALATIANS 3:24; 4:4, 5 _____

9. By what priceless blood has our great High Priest entered heaven for us once for all?

9:12; I PETER 1:18, 19 _____

10. What has this precious blood obtained for all true believers?

9:12 _____

11. What actually removes from our consciences the burden of sin?

9:14 _____

12. Do our good works in any way contribute to the removal of this burden?

9:14; ISAIAH 64:6a; EPHESIANS 2:8, 9 _____

"Without shedding of blood is no remission" of sin (9:15-28)

13. What statement shows that the death of Christ redeems believers who were under the law as well as those under grace?

9:15 _____

_____

14. What was necessary to bring the new covenant into force?

9:16, 17 _____

15. What was absolutely necessary for our salvation?

9:22 _____

16. Where is Christ now?

9:24 _____

17. What did Christ do when He appeared on earth the first time, and how did He do it?

9:26 _____

18. What one word settles the eternal permanence of Christ's work on the cross?

9:26, 28 _____

19. For those who do not take Christ as Saviour, what is certain after death?

9:27 _____

20. For whom are believers in Christ looking now?

9:28 _____

Some Christians may lack full instruction regarding the Lord's second coming. Yet the Bride awaits her Bridegroom's coming to take her to the home He has prepared for her. The Lord's Supper points backward to the cross and forward to the Lord's return. (See I CORINTHIANS 11:26.)

Christ—
the Perfect Sacrifice

10:1-39 _____

"One sacrifice for sins forever" (10:12)

Chapter 10 proceeds to show that what the sacrifices offered under the law could not do—give perfect peace of conscience and access to a holy God—the sacrifice of Christ can and does do for the believer.

The sacrifice of Christ once for all (10:1-18)

1. What were the Levitical ceremonies under the law?

10:1a. _____

_____, and *not* _____

_____

2. What were the repeated annual sacrifices unable to do?

10:1b. _____

3. How do we know those animal sacrifices were unable to purge, or purify, the offerers?

10:2 _____

4. What was the purpose of making those sacrifices annually?

10:3 _____

5. What was it impossible for the blood of animals to do?

10:4 _____

6. In order for God to make it possible for His Son to offer an effective sacrifice for sins, what did He do?

10:5 _____

7. When the Lord Jesus came into the world, what did He say to His Father?

10:7; PSALM 40:7, 8 _____

8. What was the basic purpose of the Son in taking a human body?

10:10 _____

9. What does the offering of the body of Jesus Christ accomplish for us who believe?

10:10 _____

"Sanctified" means "set apart," and here the idea is that the believer is set apart by God for Himself.

10. What can no sacrifice other than that of Christ ever do?

10:11 _____

11. What phrase shows that the work of the Aaronic priest was never finished?

10:11 _____

12. What shows that Christ's sacrificial work is forever finished?

10:12 _____

13. What did Christ accomplish by His one offering for sins?

10:14 _____

14. Since the believer's sins have been put away forever, what will God never do regarding our sins?

10:17 _____

15. Where there is remission of sins, what can there no longer be?

10:18 _____

Exhortation to steadfastness of faith (10:19-39)

The remainder of the epistle emphasizes the need for steadfastness of faith in view of our Lord's being who He is, and doing what He does.

16. What privilege now belongs to the believer?

10:19 _____

17. What does the veil represent?

10:20 _____

18. In view of the Lord's faithfulness, what should **we do**?

10:23 _____

19. To what two things should believers provoke, or stimulate, one another?

10:24 _____

20. In this same connection, it is important for us to do what?

10:25 _____

Note that in 10:26-31 the writer pauses to warn all Hebrews professing to have entered the sphere of the new covenant that if they should revert to Judaism—as a result of the pressure put upon them by unbelievers (10:32-34)—they would be utterly without a sacrifice for sin. Compare 10:26, ". . . there remaineth no more sacrifice for sins," with 10:12, 14, 18. Remember that the person described here is *not* a backslider who has fallen by the way. Rather, this is a hypothetical case of a Hebrew who returned to Judaism with its blood sacrifices—an open insult to God, in view of the final Sacrifice already offered. This passage is similar to that in HEBREWS 6:4-6.

21. If one should sin willfully (compare 10:29) after having received such full knowledge of the truth, in what position would he find himself?

10:26, 27 (last clause of verse 26) _____

_____

22. How was an Old Testament Jew punished if he despised the Law of Moses?

10:28 _____

23. In 10:29 how does the writer describe the action of a Jew who knew the truths of the new covenant and returned to the old? He would be

a. treading _____

b. counting _____

c. doing _____

24. What did some of the Jews do after Pentecost, in spite of the signs, wonders and miracles attesting the deity of Christ?

ACTS 2:43; 7:51 _____

In 10:32-39, note the comfort and encouragement addressed to true believers in Christ. Compare HABAKKUK 2:3, 4 with HEBREWS 10:37, 38. The quotation from the prophet, "The just shall live by faith," introduces the great faith chapter of the Bible—HEBREWS 11.

You have now finished the study of some basic truths in Hebrews 9 and 10. Review these by rereading the questions and your written answers. If you are uncertain about an answer, reread the Scripture text given and check your answer. Then take the following test to see how well you have understood and remembered the important truths you have studied.

In the right-hand margin write "True" or "False" after each of the following statements.

1. The chief article of furniture in the Holiest of all was the brazen altar.

2. The lid of the ark was called the mercy seat?

3. The shedding of Jesus' blood actually opened the way into the Holiest of all in heaven.

4. Our good works contribute somewhat to the removal of our sins.

5. Christ is now in heaven, appearing in the presence of God for us.

6. The animal sacrifices of the Old Testament purged the offerers of their sins.

7. When Jesus came into the world, He said, "Here am I, send me."

8. We are sanctified through the offering of the body of Jesus Christ.

9. The work of the Aaronic priest was never finished. _____

10. We are urged in HEBREWS 10 to stimulate one another to preach the gospel.

Turn to page 64 and check your answers.

The Victory of Faith

11:1-40

"Without faith it is impossible to please . . . God." (11:6)

HEBREWS 11 summons the people of God to a life of unwavering confidence in Him. To encourage the Hebrew Christians in the midst of persecution and trial, the Holy Spirit brings before them brief reminders of Old Testament believers whose memory they loved. All of these had conquered by taking God at His word. (Compare ACTS 27:25.) We too may conquer: "This is the victory that overcometh the world, even our faith" (I JOHN 5:4).

The exercise of faith (11:1, 6)

1. What is said of faith in 11:1?

a. _____

b. _____

2. What two requirements of one who comes to God are stated in 11:6?

a. _____

b. _____

The victory of Old Testament believers—"by faith" (11:2-40)

The word "elders" (11:2) is, literally, "ancients," used here as a term of honor. But note also "we" and "us" in 11:3 and 40.

3. According to 11:3, what does faith teach us?

_____

4. Did Abel have faith in the Saviour to come?

11:4; 12:24; MATTHEW 23:35 _____

5. Write the names of all those to whom the words "by faith" or "through faith" are applied in HEBREWS 11. (Note also the many others included in 11:33 and 39.)

_____

_____

6. How did Enoch please God?

11:5 _____

7. To what extent must a seeker after God apply himself to the search?

11:6; JEREMIAH 29:13 _____

8. How does Peter describe Noah?

II PETER 2:5 _____

9. How did Noah (or anyone) become an heir of the righteousness of God?

11:7 _____

10. What did Abraham do by faith?

11:8 _____

11. What did Abraham look for, by faith?

11:10 _____

12. What did faith enable Sara to do?

11:11 _____

13. What supreme test of faith came to the patriarchs before they received the things God promised?

11:13 _____

14. How did the faith and hopes of the patriarchs reach beyond mere temporal blessings?

11:15, 16 _____

15. What severe test was given Abraham's faith?

11:17, 18 _____

16. Since God had promised that the Messiah was to come through Isaac (GENESIS 21:12), what did Abraham's faith enable him to believe?

11:19 _____

17. According to 11:20-22, did Isaac, Jacob and Joseph believe such promises as those in GENESIS 12:1-3; 15:13, 14; 26:4; 28:14?

Compare GALATIANS 3:8. _____

"Time would fail" (11:32) to list the proof of faith in Moses' parents, Moses himself and all the others named and unnamed in 11:23-40. But note especially the references to "the reproach of Christ" (11:26), even though Moses lived about 1500 B.C.; the Passover (11:28; compare I CORINTHIANS 5:7); a resurrection hope (11:35). Can you add to the list?

52

18. Even though some of those mentioned in this chapter had notable faults recorded against them, what does God say about them?

11:39; compare 10:17 _____

A summary of the requirements of faith

We may well examine our own hearts in the light of the faith of these Old Testament believers, as summarized in the following requirements of faith: belief in God's existence (v. 6); trust in His promises (v. 6); obedience to His guidance (v. 8); dependence on His faithfulness (v. 11); acknowledgment of His ability (v. 19); response to His presence (v. 27); confidence in divine revelation (v. 39).

The Chastisement of God

12:1-29

"Whom the Lord loveth he chasteneth." (12:6)

Keep in mind the connection between chapters 11 and 12. The faith chapter has brought before us an array of men and women who in times past conquered through faith. It could be said of each one, as it is written of Abel: "He being dead yet speaketh." These heroes of faith lived before the incarnation of the Lord Jesus, before the cross, before Christ ascended as High Priest; yet they trusted in the face of all discouragements. How much more should *we* believe God!

Exhortation to patience in trial (12:1-13)

1. What two things are we to lay aside as we run the Christian race?

12:1 _____

2. To whom are we to look as we run?

12:2 _____

While we are to cherish the memory of the saints in heaven, walking with firmer step because of their faith, our eyes are to be fixed on the Lord Jesus only.

3. What word does Paul use to describe a hindrance to others in our lives?

I Corinthians 8:8, 9 _____

For the sake of serving God effectively, we may have to lay aside many good things—weights which would consume too much of our time, means and energy—or be stumbling blocks to others.

4. What must we continually do regarding sin in our lives?

I John 1:9 _____

5. What quality do we need very much?

12:1 _____

6. What two things about Jesus make Him the One to whom to look?

12:2a _____

7. What is the source of faith?

Romans 10:17 _____

8. How is the keeping power of God brought to us?

I Peter 1:5 _____

9. What did the Lord Jesus endure that should serve as the supreme example of faith?

12:2 _____

10. Since it is sometimes costly to maintain a testimony for Christ, what should we do?

12:3 _____

11. What indicates that the Hebrew Christians had not yet suffered extensive martyrdom?

12:4 _____

12. Though we may be called upon to endure suffering for His sake, how should we regard it?

12:5 _____

Chastening is education through discipline, intended to produce improvement. It has been called "child training."

13. What does such chastening or discipline indicate?

12:6; PROVERBS 3:12; 13:24 _____

14. If we were without chastening or chastisement, what would that indicate as to our relationship to God?

12:8 _____

15. If we expect to live the Christian life in subjection to God our Father, what should we gladly accept?

12:9 _____

16. For what purpose does our heavenly Father chasten us?

12:10 _____

To chasten means to make chaste or pure.

17. What does chastening, properly accepted, accomplish?

12:11 _____

18. In view of the blessing which trial is intended to produce, what should we do?

12:12, 13 _____

Warning against trifling with God (12:14-29)

In the rest of the chapter the writer of the epistle again takes up the note of warning against trifling with the things of the new covenant. This is illustrated by Esau, who sold his birthright. "When he afterward desired to inherit the blessing, he was rejected; for he found no place for a change of mind in his father, though he sought it diligently with tears" (12:17, A.S.V.).

The Holy Spirit now contrasts the heavenly realities of the new covenant with the conditions under the Sinai covenant. He shows that Sinai is no place for the sinner, but that the real way to God is the way of "a green hill . . . without a city wall," where Jesus, the Mediator of the new covenant, laid down the redemption price for every sinner.

19. Because we, as believers in Christ, receive "a kingdom that cannot be shaken" (12:28, A.S.V.), what are we urged to do?

_____

_____

20. What fact about "our God" is to be kept in mind?

12:29 _____

Remember that destruction is but the occasional and accidental effect of fire, caused by disregard of the laws of fire. Its real and constant task for believers is to quicken, cherish and bless. God is love; therefore He can burn with indignation at evil. One can realize His love for sinners only when he sees Him in the light of His blazing wrath against sin, giving His only begotten Son to die for us.

The Unchanging Christ

13:1-25

_____

> "Jesus Christ the same yesterday, and today, and forever." (13:8)

"The final statement in chapter 12 refers to our God as a consuming fire. Now in 13:1-6 we have the things which the holy fire of the divine abhorrence of evil will not consume."—Max I. Reich. And by the grace of the unchanging Christ every believer in Him may have these virtues.

A call to Christian living (13:1-6)

1. What is true faith expected to produce in the Christian life?

13:1 _____

2. What is one excellent way of manifesting the love of Christ?

13:2; compare I PETER 4:9 _____

_____

3. What is another excellent way of manifesting the love of Christ?

13:3; MATTHEW 25:34-36 _____

_____

4. What is God's view of marriage?

13:4a _____

5. How does Paul characterize any doctrine forbidding marriage?

I TIMOTHY 4:1-3 _____

6. Whose sanction of marriage does the Lord Jesus cite?

MATTHEW 19:3-6 _____

7. What is God's view regarding violators of the laws of marriage?

13:4b _____

8. With what should we be content?

13:5a _____

9. Why should no Christian ever be covetous?

13:5b, 6; PHILIPPIANS 4:19 _____

The call to complete separation from Judaism (13:7-17)

Verse 7 (A.S.V.) reads, "Remember them that had the rule over you," that is, formerly; verse 17, "Obey them that have the rule over you." Way's Translation calls these leaders "spiritual guides."

10. What quality in our spiritual guides are we to follow?

13:7 _____.

11. What truth about Jesus Christ should keep us from being carried away with strange doctrines?

13:8; compare 13:9 _____.

---

12. Who is able to build us up spiritually and by what means?

Acts 20:32 _____

13. What answer can we give to those who object that Christians have no altar?

13:10 _____.

14. Who is the Christian's Sacrifice?

I Corinthians 5:7b _____

15. If Jews who believed in Jesus Christ were excommunicated from the synagogue, of what might this remind them?

13:11, 12 _____

16. If we are under reproach for being identified with Christ crucified, what should we do?

13:13 _____

17. Meanwhile, what comfort do we have?

13:14 _____

18. What is the sacrifice we now have to offer God as we "make confession to his name" (13:15, A.S.V.)?

_____

19. What sacrifices besides praise are pleasing to God?

13:16 _____

20. Who produces in us even the desire to do good?

Philippians 2:13 _____

Conclusion of the epistle (13:18-25)

The writer's request for prayer, the benediction and personal greetings conclude the Epistle to the Hebrews. Every Christian should memorize the benediction (13:20, 21) for the comfort and hope it gives.

As the Good Shepherd, Christ died for us (JOHN 10:11); as the Great Shepherd, the risen Lord ever lives as our great High Priest (13:20); as the Chief Shepherd, He will appear in glory (I PETER 5:4). He can and will enable us even now to "do his will" (13:21) if we give Him first place in our hearts. To Him "be glory forever and ever" (13:21).

You have now finished this study of the Epistle to the Hebrews—and, in particular, chapters 11, 12 and 13. Review the truths learned in these three chapters by rereading the questions and your written answers. If you are not sure about an answer, reread the Scripture text given and check your answer. Then take the following test to see how well you understand and remember the important truths you have studied.

In the right-hand margin write "True" or "False" after each of the following statements.

1. One requirement of a person who comes to God is that he believe that God is. _____

2. By faith Abel offered a more excellent sacrifice than Cain. _____

3. In HEBREWS 11, the Holy Spirit mentions many faults of the Old Testament believers. _____

4. HEBREWS 11 tells us that Isaac looked for a city "whose builder and maker is God." _____

5. We are told to lay aside both weights and sin. _____

6. Chastening indicates that God no longer loves us. _____

7. Our God is a consuming fire. _____

8. HEBREWS 13 tells us that marriage is not always honorable. _____

9. Paul says the Christian who puts God first will be blessed with much prosperity. _____

10. Christ is the Christian's Sacrifice. _____

Turn to page 64 and check your answers.

Suggestions for class use

1. The class teacher may wish to tear this page from each workbook as the answer key is on the reverse side.

2. The teacher should study the lesson first, filling in the blanks in the workbook. He should be prepared to give help to the class on some of the harder places in the lesson. He should also take the self-check tests himself, check his answers with the answer key and look up any question answered incorrectly.

3. Class sessions can be supplemented by the teacher's giving a talk or leading a discussion on the subject to be studied. The class could then fill in the workbook together as a group, in teams, or individually. If so desired by the teacher, however, this could be done at home. The self-check tests can be done as homework by the class.

4. The self-check tests can be corrected at the beginning of each class session. A brief discussion of the answers can serve as review for the previous lesson.

5. The teacher should motivate and encourage his students. Some public recognition might well be given to class members who successfully complete this course.

Moody Press, a ministry of the Moody Bible Institute, is designed for education, evangelization and edification. If we may assist you in knowing more about Christ and the Christian life, please write us without obligation to: Moody Press, c/o MLM, Chicago, Illinois 60610.

answer key
to self-check tests

Be sure to look up any questions you answered incorrectly.

Q gives the number of the test *question*.

A gives the correct *answer*.

R *refers* you back to the lesson number and the question number in that lesson for the correct answer.

Mark with an "x" your wrong answers, if any.

TEST 1			TEST 2			TEST 3		
Q	A	R	Q	A	R	Q	A	R
1	F	1-2	1	T	3-2	1	T	5-1
2	T	1-6	2	F	3-4	2	F	5-3
3	T	1-9	3	F	3-14	3	F	5-5
4	T	1-15	4	T	3-10	4	F	5-8
5	F	1-22	5	F	3-29	5	T	5-14
6	F	2-17	6	F	4-1	6	T	6-1
7	T	2-4	7	F	4-8	7	T	6-2
8	T	2-7	8	T	4-9	8	F	6-15
9	F	2-10	9	F	4-13	9	F	6-7
10	T	2-15	10	T	4-22	10	T	6-12

TEST 4			TEST 5			TEST 6		
Q	A	R	Q	A	R	Q	A	R
1	F	7-1	1	F	9-1	1	T	11-2
2	T	7-3	2	T	9-2	2	T	11-4
3	F	7-7	3	T	9-6	3	F	11-18
4	F	7-9	4	F	9-12	4	F	11-11
5	T	7-17	5	T	9-16	5	T	12-1
6	F	8-2	6	F	10-3	6	F	12-13
7	T	8-6	7	F	10-7	7	T	12-20
8	T	8-10	8	T	10-9	8	F	13-4
9	T	8-15	9	T	10-11	9	F	13-9
10	F	8-20	10	F	10-19	10	T	13-14

How well did you do?

0-1 wrong answers on any one test—excellent work

2-3 wrong answers on any one test—review these items carefully

4 or more wrong answers—restudy the lesson before going on to the next one

A Godly Interruption

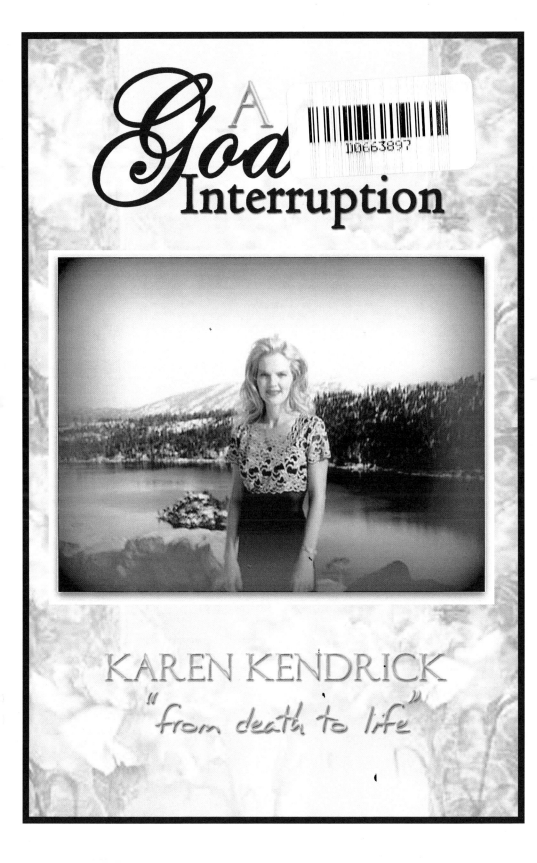

KAREN KENDRICK
"from death to life"

For Book Signing or Speaking engagements
Karen Kendrick Ministries
C/0 Miracle Tabernacle
P.O. Box 3927
Bay St. Louis, Ms 39521
www.karenkendrick.org
kendrickkaren@gmail.com

LEGACY
PUBLISHING HOUSE

A DIVISION OF REMNANT PUBLISHING

Published by;
Legacy House Publishing
Dr. J. S. Vaughn
all publishing rights reserved

The
KAREN KENDRICK

MIRACLE STORY

a story of hope

a journey of faith

a book of mercy & grace

QUITE SIMPLY, KAREN KENDRICK SHOULD NOT BE
ALIVE TO HAVE WRITTEN THIS BOOK.
HOWEVER, WITH THE POWER OF
THE SPOKEN WORD OF GOD
Even Death Had to Obey

Dedication

This book, which I call God's book... ordered by Him...I would like to dedicate to my mother and my father; Rev. Frank & Wanda Kendrick. Not only are they my parents, the most amazing parents in the world . . . but they also serve as faithful pastors of Miracle Tabernacle, Waveland, Ms

Special Thanks to Shane Vaughn . . . Thank you for your obedience to God and for the hours of work you've put into this project. Without you, this book would not have been written. God hand picked you with the talents and gifts He's given you to be used mightly in the planting of this seed that will reap a harvest around the world.

The Kendrick Family

Myself, Mom, Dad & My Brother Kevin

Chapters

INTRODUCTION — page 17

THEY WHISPERED A NAME — page 25

MY DAUGHTER IS NOT DEAD — page 35

ANGELS IN THE ROOM — page 39

THE SCARS OF MY BATTLE — page 37

THE 8TH DAY - RETURNED TO LIFE — page 51

EVERYTHING NEW — page 59

MIRACLES TODAY — page 67

Dedication

Also, I would like to dedicate this book to my grandmother Helen Thornhill. She has since passed from this earth but while here not only was she my grandmother but one of my best friends. She always believed in me and encouraged me to be the best I could be.

Foreward
by; Dr. Saundra Seale

God alone knows how to interrupt time and space to release a mighty miracle.

Through the pages of this book you are now holding you will be excited to read one account after the other as our heavenly Father does a wonderful life changing miracle.

Karen is a fine example of an awesome woman on a mission to share the miraculous and to challenge the reader to stir up their faith to believe that their God is more than enough. As you read this account of Gods work as He uses this beautiful woman of God to walk through the storms to her victory, know the same can be done for you!!!

Dr. Saundra Jones Seale Ph.d.
President & Author
Crisis Recovery Institite

Foreward

by; Pastor. Frank Kendrick

From a little girl God has chosen her; Prophets prophesied over her that she would be used of God when she was just a child. The enemy has tried to take her away from us a few years ago even to the point of death at *Tulane Medical Center* in New Orleans; no doubt the enemy had his gang cheering trying to disprove Gods call on her life.

Every single organ of her body was no longer functioning. Medical science said when she was admitted that IT WAS OVER! They said TOO LATE! But, down deep in the inner recesses of her body, basically a corpse, there was A CALL. That call is more powerful than all the intelligence of men or the powers of this world.

That call followed her even when her skin was dying and falling from her corpse of a body. During all of this people in uniforms; both nurses and doctors, kept shaking their heads in amazement because EVERY person who ever entered that hospital in that condition previously all left as a "Memory" but never as a miracle.

Everyone but God was surprised! He is bigger than even the love her mother and I had for our beautiful little daughter even from a baby girl. What happened next - The Miracle wasn't because of our hurting, nor Gods desire to relieve us of that hurting, but rather because of HIS CALL upon her life and her unfilled destiny! The great stir in Tulane Medical Center; the great mystery of this dead girl being brought back to life caused her physician to state emphatically that I DIDN'T DO ANYTHING! He simply pointed his finger upward toward the sky.

All of the nurses who attended to Karen, who had all seen such a hopeless situation; many of them shouted around her room at this miracle of biblical proportions. All of a sudden and I MEAN SUDDENLY every organ went from negative to positive suddenly EVERY ORGAN WAS ALIVE! Her old dead skin began peeling off and brand new baby skin begin to form over her emaciated body.

I remember well that many of the new interns who were training were brought into Karen's room with their note pads as they heard the story they would all stand in amazement at this medically unexplainable miracle. The administrator knew perfectly well the hopeless condition of Karen's body and when she came in and saw Karen she also began literally shouting around her room - this was an undeniable miracle.

In just a short amount of time Karen regained ALL of her strength and even more ; the strength of youth! She began running miles and miles every day without any medication whatsoever. But, it was not simply her physical strength that returned but now her life had new meaning and purpose.

Now, EVERYTHING she does, everything she talks about HE's involved. This call of God is soooooo powerful. Great things ARE GOING to happen in her ministry. Why not? God brought her back to share His healing power with the world and I KNOW that this is about to happen.

by: Rev. Frank Kendrick
Pastor
Miracle Tabernacle
Waveland, Ms

Acknowledgement

DARRYL HALL, PASTOR OF CHRIST CATHEDRAL, BILOXI, MS - *for hearing my mother scream at Hancock Medical Center "My Daughters not dead" and running to her rescue and Speaking the Word for her to roll the windows of her car down while she was praying...you took her hand and agreed with her that "this situation is being taken care of" You have spoken words of encouragement to my parents ever since that day.*

REV. PAUL SPRINGER - *for caring enough to leave the demands of your responsibilities and supporting our family and for your prayers.*

MILDRED MORSE - *for your prayers and knowing your personality; even in the midst of this storm you probably managed to make the ones around you laugh.*

CHERYL MORSE - *for praying for me even though you couldn't make yourself come to see me; you were there*

SHARON RIBALDO - *for being there with prayer and support*

My Uncle, Charles Blount - *for your prayers and knowing your personality, you probably helped ease the tension with your laughter.*

My Aunt, Renee' Blount - *for your support of prayer, love and concern*

Albert & Corrine Beyl - *for being loyal in prayer & your outpouring of love and support*

Corrine Boyd - *for your outpouring of love and support*

Glenda Bates - *for your love and concern*

Keith Kinchen - *for coming to the hospital and supporting my parents and son*

Rachael Kinchen - *for being at the hospital right away...even in the coma...I heard your giggle...you telling me "let's go get coffee K.K"*

My Brother, Kevin Kendrick - *for being the best brother in the world as always...being there for me through every good and bad time*

Kathy Kendrick - *for your alway present love and your refusal to give up on anything*

My Son, Kent Kinchen - *for being the best son a mother could ask for. For sharing the vision that God gave you while I was in the coma that I would run around the nurses station and for inspiring faith*

Barry Kinchen - *for coming to the hospital and praying for me and supporting our son and my parents*

MY COUSIN, LORI LEGG - *for being the watchdog over every nurse, doctor and person to make sure I was being treated right*

MY UNCLE, HARRY PARKE - *for being your ever-present wonderful, praying self*

MY AUNT, JEAN PARKE - *for never failing to not let us down when the chips were down; for being there and for your prayers and support.*

MY AUNT, FRANCIS BASS - *for being who you always are....there*

MY UNCLE, REV. WAYNE BASS - *for being there with strength and prayer*

MY AUNT, DEBBIE FRAZIER - *for taking charge in situations going on around when others were too distressed to think straight*

DIANNA TROYER - *for being present almost immediatly when you heard of this*

NORMA BLOUNT - *for your prayers and help and support of the family*

MY UNCLE, REV. LLOYD BLOUNT - *for always beleiving in me; for going home when hearing of this....crying out to God, begging for Him to let me live*

MY AUNT, REGINA BLOUNT - *for being there and seeng past this; you saw where I would be after this was over....my destiny*

ELEONER KINCHEN - *Wow . . .I was told how much love you gave towards me; thank you*

DARENDA ROBERTSON - *for being the little prayer warrior that you always are*

JOBY BURAS - *for driving in and going out of your way...you spoke Words over me that we would once again sing together in church and we did*

CHRISTINE GARCIA - *for being one of the rocks of our church...no matter what's happened in your life I can always count on your for prayer*

DALE & MARGIE AMAZSON - *for coming to my room even before the hospital and lying next to me in my bed and praying over me*

SCARLET BLOUNT - *for instructing the nurses to put socks on my feet because they were cold*

SUSAN PERRIN - *for being there and loving on Kent, Mom and Dad*

JOINER FAMILY - *for being supportive in prayer*

DAN RUSH - *for being such a friend to my parents and being there for them in love and prayer*

CHAD BARNETTE - *for come with Dale & Margie to my bedside even before I left home*

JUDY GUICE - *for taking the time to place me into the World Network of Prayer; even when your husband Steve was so ill*

HARDY & JILL JONES - *for the intercession and your unstoppable faith and for believing that this mountain WOULD be moved! Also, thanks for the ride:)*

MEMBERS OF MIRACLE TABERNACLE - *for constantly praying and calling at all hours for updates*

My family at my parents 50th wedding anniversary

Introduction

I've often wondered what the Bible would be like without the story of Lazarus. I remember listening with childhood wonder as my Daddy would preach in our beloved home church, Miracle Tabernacle about Mary and Martha and their tears of sadness being replaced with rapturous tears of joy when that carpenter from Galilee said "*Come Forth*". I often asked to my self; What if someone had simply forgotten to write that story down for us?

EVERYDAY
AROUND THE WORLD
GOD DOES MIRACLES

Millions of people around the world experience a dynamic lifting of their faith when hearing about Lazarus; this simple man from Bethany with just a simple life; much like you and me. Generations of Christians have loved hearing about his being called back from the chains of death in that divine moment of what I've come to term as a GOD INTERRUPTION. The simplicity of this story would be used for thousands of years to illustrate the majesty of Jesus. But, someone could have just ignored that gentle prompting of the Holy Spirit and "*forgotten*" or even worse "*refused*" to write the story; imagine the travesty of such forgetfulness.

When God gave me a mandate to write about my own modern day Lazarus miracle for you to read; it wasn't an easy command. Life is busy and sometimes the majesty of the memory drifts away on the winds of time and we simply forget; not out of lack of appreciation but simply because life moves on and demands that you move with it. However, there are some moments in life that have eternal meaning and must never be placed in the vaults of memories but rather placed on the pedestal of perpituty for the glory of God. In a world that screams out "God doesn't care" in a society that preaches "God is dead or not concerned about your life" there must come forth THE TRUTH and THE TRUTH is given as a public testimony in this book that Jesus Christ still loves to do the impossible. Jesus Christ is still the same and He lives and He loves and He heals and He cares. My story... or rather His story that he brought to pass in my life is not an ancient relic that you cannot verify.

This miracle is not relegated to thousands of years ago and only to be accepted by faith. No, my story happened in your lifetime; my healing didn't take place in biblical days but in YOUR DAY! Once you read these pages and once you read about a virtual modern-day Lazarus story of biblical proportions then I believe you'll understand why God whispered these divine directives into my spirit when He continues to press me to WRITE THE BOOK.

Everyday around the world God does miracles! There are unnoticed and uncredited GOD INTERRUPTIONS in the lives of people at all times and sadly those miracles escape our minds and someone forgets to tell the story and the masses of people continue believing the lies of Satan that *GOD IS NOT INVOLVED* in the lives of people. It is for this very reason that I sit at my laptop now and steal away from the demands of my life because I have a story to tell you about the goodness of that gentleman from Galilee; the lover of my soul, Jesus Christ

I n the month of November everything is pretty much dying along the beautiful and picturesque Gulf Coast of Mississippi; the place that I call home.

All of the foliage and flora of spring is being put away by Mother Nature. In her haste for the seasons change, the lilies and the bursting azaleas are replaced by the plunging leaves and the crisp of fall. Death is literally in the air as all of nature prepares to survive the dark months of winter.

Hardly did I know that those very whispers of winter death would begin blowing into my own life; never could I have expected what the following months and years would hold for me. How was I to know that this little sheltered southern girl would soon be given up to the cold breath of winters death in the dismal rooms of *Tulane Medical Center* in New Orleans, La; to leave behind my only child, Kent, my parents, family, friends, dreams, and surely my unfulfilled destiny.

No one could have convinced me that in just a few days my life would be divinely interrupted and one of the greatest miracles of biblical proportions would be forced upon me. Hardly, did I understand then that God in His perfect knowledge would prove Himself to be my Lily in deaths valley and that through it all He would become more beautiful to me than anything or anyone I've ever known. He; my Creator, would become my personal escort on my journey as I would soon walk to the gates of hell and literally be in the presence of the great keeper of those gates; Satan himself.

Like all southern belles; I had my measured life, my leisurely, dignified and sedate life all perfectly planned out. Well, I did in my dreams anyhow! Unhurried and unrushed I graced my way through the ways of the world and through the methods of the masses as I took "*humble*" pride in my independence and my modest success. I fell perfectly in line with the demands of society and blended with the landscape of life.

So, why would life wish to pick on me? Had I harmed anyone or done anything to deserve the indescribable torture that I would soon endure?. More importantly why would God allow my destruction? After all, I was the child of spiritual giants and I had been a believer all of my life.

Far from perfect but try as I might I couldn't think of a person I had ever harmed.

The why of it all is the beauty of my story! People always use this famous phrase "*If I knew then what I know now*" Well, for me if I had known then that it would take a divine interruption of my life tobring me into the relationship that I now have with my creator then I would have stood in line to experience the suffering, pain, and destruction.

The old personality and the old will of Karen Kendrick absolutely died, she (that personality) was not resurrected. She was a woman with her own dreams and desires her own selfish motives and agendas. But when I physically arose from my hospital bed more than my body was resurrected; my life of supernatural faith was born! Today, I have ran past the walls of mans ideas and mans ways of *"Experiencing God"* and I have flung myself completely into a trust walk with my Creator. Greater than anything you will read in this book; greater than my physical healing which is beyond words, you must experience along with me my spiritual healing, my journey from " religion" to an "intimate relationship" of daily trust and walking by faith.

GOD is more than a word; more than a theological concept or a generic term . . but rather HE IS EVERYTHING. Since my journey began in the year 2009 I have learned to walk with His voice alone and my life has grown into a life of total surrender thanks to a divine GOD INTERRUPTION in my life. Sometimes what seems like destruction is nothing more than an interruption when God has to stop the act of the play that you've devised. Sometimes, to save you from your own ultimate destruction He must step in and rearrange everything to bring you back to the purpose of your life.

SOMETIMES WHAT SEEMS LIKE DESTRUCTION IS REALLY A GOD INTERRUPTION

This is exactly what happened to me in the summer of 2009. In the next few chapters you will take an intimate look inside of my transition; you will see inside the cocoon of isolation and obscurity that God placed me in to reshape me; to re-create me; to transform me from the Karen that I had created to the one that He desired to work through. The process was hard and lonely and believe me I kicked and fought and begged for deliverance at times. However, little then did I understand that at the end of this wilderness experience God would become my only thoughts rather than just my afterthoughts. Only then when He was the priority would the desires of my heart be granted to me. Only then would I receive all of His promises. God had to prove to me that true happiness didn't come from things but rather through a complete surrender of my will to His Lordship.

YOU MUST HAVE THE "SPIRIT OF EXPECTANCY" AT ALL TIMES WHILE YOUR IN THAT VERY UNCOMFORTABLE PLACE KNOWN AS "THE WAITING"

I can take absolutely no credit for praying myself through this valley. I can say with certainty that every single day and night of my life, I have had a mother and a father that have prayed for me without fail. They have never "*thrown in the towel*" toward giving up on me no matter what. They have been my *rock of Gilbrater* in the mighty Mediterranean seas of destruction that have beaten against me.

If I had known then what today would be like I wouldn't change anything. Today, I have come to know the reality of God rather than the religions of God. He has become my strength

If you actually want "mountains" to be moved in your life; to see the impossible become possible; to actually see greater things happen than you even dreamed possible.....you must have "CRAZY": faith that doesn't even make sense to the human mind; truly believing God can do absolutely anything and He's unlimited in His power and

'*Knowing*" that He's hearing you and is going to answer. You must have the "*Spirit of expectancy*" at all times while your in that very uncomfortable place known as "the waiting." This type of faith is not free it comes through the trials and testings of your faith. However, if you truly desire this faith then you will be allowed the opportunties to develop this faith. Just a few times of seeing how perfectly God always works things out will cause you to absolutely believe.

At the start of my journey in completely seeking to "*know Him*", God carried me along as a baby. He began to teach me "*His voice*", and "*His character*". He taught me "Him" in order to "know Him" and become intimate with Him. This is called TRUE RELATIONSHIP. He taught me how this is priority before graduating to any other level spiritually. For me to have a chance in finding my destiny, what I was put on this earth for, I had to "KNOW HIM" so he could carry me there as only he can do.

In the "*knowing*" I had to realize His unlimited power and to learn to have the faith that moves Him and therefore moves the impossible. He taught me faith through many tests and how these tests bring forth strength. Test after test,and more strength each time would solidify a spiritual foundation in me that is forever unshakable. I have learned that we cannot live by: *The seeing of the eye or the hearing of the ear but only by the knowing of the now!*

Chapter One

I wasn't there so I can only tell you what I was told! This story is actually my mother's story, my father's story and my son's. They are the ones who suffered the torment of my death more than I; they cried the tears, prayed the prayers, and endured the torment.

While I lay unconscious in the cold clutches of death they were at the death watch helpless in the eyes of man but working in that mysterious place of prayer that the world knows so little about.

HERE IS THE PART I DO REMEMBER.

Meet the two rocks of my life; Mom and Dad

Katrina; a storm of storms had decided to wreak havoc upon our little sleepy hamlet of Waveland, Ms, situated just outside of New Orleans, La along the meandering and graceful, beach-lined roads of the Gulf coast. My mother and Father who have faithfully served as Pastors at Miracle Tabernacle for over thirty years were caught completely unaware when this horrible mistress of the sea, Katrina, tore through their quiet life and claimed for herself what belonged to them.

Their home that they had worked so many years for now lay in scattered shambles beneath their feet; the church they had built with blood, sweat and tears was only a memory washed away in the unforgiving tides of the Gulf of Mexico. Yet, day and night, they served our little community of pitiful souls who walked around in bewilderment as they tried to comprehend how they would ever put their lives back together. But never complaining Mom and Dad did all they've ever done; they served.

In their loss they gave and in their tears they poured their lives out to others. The members of their church leaned upon my broken parents for strength and strength is what they gave; not their own strength but His strength.

Surely, the merciless and ruthless, hard-hearted winds of Katrina and the hungry voracious waves of the Gulf would have been the greatest storm in my family's life, this without a doubt had to be their storm of the century. However, we could have never dreamed that there were greater winds yet to blow, there were grander waves of sorrow yet to roll into our already shattered lives; The Kendrick Family would soon fight our greatest battle; one greater than even an angry mother nature ever could unleash .

It was a day of Celebration; the storm had passed. The dark skies had turned to blue, the season of death and trauma had been pushed away by the return of life; the family home had been triumphantly rebuilt, the church was restored, now better than before…… ..The birds sang a new song and The Kendrick Family had gathered on this day; Nov 1st, 2008 to rejoice, to dance in the rain of our restoration.

As we gathered; Mom, Dad, Kevin, Kent and myself, mother's heart was filled with joy as any mothers heart would be because the home was now ready for her little family to enjoy the Thanksgiving and Christmas seasons. There would be reasons to give thanks and there would be peace on our little part of the earth. Life could return to the safe sanctity of its normalcy. Together as a family we had conquered the storm; ridden the waves and scaled the mountain of tragedy; life was returning to some semblance of normalcy and of course, I being the life of the party, Karen was going to be right in the middle of the festive gala.

Decorations and beautiful things are one of my passions so naturally when it came time to decorate mothers' house it was "*Karen to the rescue.*" Naturally I am head strong and not one to depend on others nor to wait around for help. I am the original "get er done" girl with the determination of a mama bulldog. Someone forgot to teach me the meaning of two words "wait" and "quit."

But, I can confess when I'm wrong when I've made a mistake and on this particular day I made a HUGE mistake. The lovely mirror that I just had to find a place for was so adorably beautiful and I just had to get it in that perfect place that I had envisioned in my mind. But,

In New York … shopping

no one was there to help me lift it and when no one was there to help me; oh well, I grabbed it myself and wow; I had no idea how heavy this little beauty was. Months earlier I had suffered a physical setback in my nursing career. As a registered nurse I have always had to lift on heavy patients and as a result I had torn the right rotator cuff in my right shoulder; the pain was OMG!

The surgeon that had been consulted informed me that surgery would probably be necessary. In the meantime he gave me a steroid injection to help with the pain but that help didn't last very long. Finally it was so excruciating that he then prescribed the medication Lortab to control the pain just to be able to continue in my career. No one will ever understand nor would I expect them to or wish them to; the intensity of that physical pain until you have felt it. Over the months the Lortabs had come to make it bearable and on this particular day at mom's house I forgot to remind myself about my torn shoulder. But it wouldn't take anything more than one heavy mirror to send my mind spiraling back to just how intense my pain was and the unwelcomed surprise of the feeling as if my lower back had been cracked. Of course, now, I'm realizing how much more careful I should have been in waiting for help. *"If only"*.....don't you just love those *"should have, could have and would haves of life"*

This one bad decision, this one momentary lapse in judgment altered the course of my life and it is at this point that I can only relate to you what Mom has told me, what Dad has said and what Kent saw. Immediately; my parents wanted to rush me to the emergency room because my agony was so intense with this pain now shooting through my back. However, it was the weekend and being a veteran nurse I of all people understand what that means. So, I told them no and against their better judgment they submitted to my wishes when I convinced them that I would be okay.

There is no way they could have known just how much pain was wrenching my body, tearing at my muscles and convulsing my mind. I remember, just wanting out of my skin as the sweat broke and as the fear consumed my thoughts; something was very wrong, so very wrong. However, I can handle anything or so I had always believed, *"just a little bed rest and I'll be fine"*. I knew if I were to go to the ER I would be given pain medicine and I already had that. Being a nurse, I have medicated patients over and over for pain. Therefore, I thought, *"of course I can do this for my own self"*. I just wanted to do anything to keep from worrying my family and to make the pain go away; anything to get back to the celebration of our lives.

My piano since the age of four that my Dad got me. With my little friend Jayden

I remember the first one, then the second one and after that still no relief, so I took a third one. After that third Lortab I have no memory. The void in my memory took place when I began medicating the pain. I was not conscience of what I was doing but as I was later told, I must have been very aware of the pain as evidenced by my moaning, grimacing and holding onto my back. The dark shadows of the void filled my mind, the nothingness replaced my memories and I disappeared into that place of darkness where the soul seems to take a journey from the body…

I do not remember taking over two-hundred pills! How? When? Why did that happen? I have no idea. The only "proof" that it had happened was an empty bottle; which I know was full. No one had any idea that I had medicated myself for the pain. As I drifted further and further away from life on the seas of death; my precious family was clueless that I had ingested enough medication to kill a normal person in mere moments.

As far as the family knew I had been working such long hours that when I finally went to bed the stress of the job had sedated my body into a mandatory rest. Of course, mom lived in my bedroom for three days with that suspicious feeling that something was very wrong but who was she to question the registered nurse? For three days they wondered what could be wrong; clueless about the medication they simply prayed and waited. Mother rubbed my back

the entire three days. She tells how I moaned and groaned in pain while rubbing my lower back. The entire time my bloodstream was being taken over by the poison of a medication meant to be taken only in the smallest doses. It was racing through my veins shutting my body down for the moment of death. Yet, mother prayed, rubbed my back, fretted and worried. She slept in my bed for two nights watching me and refusing to sleep.

The responsibilities of the church still rested upon her as the Thanksgiving banquet was scheduled and even though she did not want to attend, she was never one to avoid her duties to the church. Reluctantly, she rushed to the church to do what must be done but she tells of knowing that something was very bad, just how bad she had no way of knowing. She asked the church to pray; they prayed. Then several of the elders of the church came to my bedside at the house and prayed for me. Hell always knows when the church is praying and therefore Satan no doubt stepped up his plan for my life.

For in just a very few short hours he would exhale the final breaths out of my dying body. But, the church WAS praying! Mom was praying; Dad was praying and the prince of darkness had his work cut out for him because God hears the prayers of righteous people. If there's anything I know and Satan knows it's the life of Frank & Wanda Kendrick. As a result of prayer there was about to be a
GOD INTERRUPTION.

It was unusually warm in the south during November of 2008 and just as unpredictable as Mississippi weather are the strategies of Satan. Little did we know that this day, Nov 3rd would mark the end of my life. It made no sense; I had been given the promises of God that my life would be used for the glory of God. I had a whole life yet to live. I had little idea that what Satan was meaning for my destruction was Gods secret plan to fulfill all of His previous promises to me. I had no idea that Gods PLAN B was actually His PLAN A the whole time. I'm reminded of that beautiful verse of scripture – "*Oh the depths of His ways, who can know them*". Satan devised my destruction and hardly could he understand that God was using him as an instrument in His own hands to bring about the greatest days of my life, these days that I now live, these days of open doors and total happiness, these days of fulfilled promises and open heavens; I had no idea that it would take my enduring those days to enjoy these days.

Mom looked down at me on the third day as she awakened from one of her brief naps while sleeping with me and something was tragically wrong. She tells of the very moment when she describes me as being completely black and blue and curled up like a "dead kitten." Pitiful and putrid I lay beside her and try as she might she couldn't awaken me. There was no moan from me, no movement, no activity, violently and yet silently over two-hundred Lortabs had now com-

pletely destroyed my organs as my body prepared to die.

When I refused to move; when the pitiful sight of my dying flesh was too much for mother to take she tells of doing something that she had never done to me. Panic stricken and filled with torment of the mind she slapped me across my face to awaken me and yet I lay unmoved; I was gone!

With the screams that only a mother in torment and agony over her child can make she released the bloodcurdling in her voice as she yelled my father's name. The moment my faithful father saw me, instincts took over and everyone in the room knew that fate had dealt her final blow. With the arms of a loving father he scooped me up and tried to make me stand yet my body stiffened the more and time nor tale will ever be able to recreate that moment of fear, that moment when you know your child is gone.

My precious son Kent ran to his grandfather's aid as they moved with gentle swiftness to rush my body to the emergency room of *Hancock Medical Center* in Waveland, MS. Resting in the solace of my mother's lap, on this November 3rd, which ironically was her birthday, no doubt drenched with the rivers of her tears, I lay there lifeless as moment by moment breath found its final escape from my gentle frame.

FRANK, she's GONE! That was the words that filled the vehicle when mom looked at me and noticed the last vestige of breath leave my body, my stomach stopping its movement surrendering to the curse of the crisis and the end of the fight. Mother told

After nursing for 20 years, my last day to clock out!

my father and son in the front seat *"She's Gone"* and that moment became immortalized in time as my family recalls the screaming out of the only name they had come to trust, the only name that they knew in the time of crisis. Together as a family they ran into that strong tower of the name of Jesus as in unison without practice and without anyone missing their timing, that name above all names ascended from their lips… JESUS…… and that friend of the friendless must have heard their call because the giver of life did once again what He did for Adam. He breathed life back into my body as my stomach resumed its rhythm.

FRANK, SHE'S GONE

But Satan would not yet yield his claim even after they whispered "the name". God only "allowed" this claim to live on because of what He had planned soon to "interrupt". But it wasn't time yet. This attack had to be allowed to continue; it had to continue where this was being allowed to be taken to. Where? To the very point of no hope; no way out; no humanly way possible to fix!

MY DAUGHTER IS NOT DEAD

Chapter Two

Our little community hospital *Hancock Medical Center* was probably ill prepared for the waves of family, friends and visitors that would soon be rushing in to face the inevitable; my death. The halls were filled with the flurry of those who had heard the devastating news and were mentally preparing to help my parents through the loss of their child; I'm forever thankful for each of them who came. It was an accepted fact that I was dead and rightly so!

As my parents rushed into the emergency room of *Hancock Medical* it was quickly determined that ALL HOPE WAS GONE. In the human minds of my loved ones as with any other family there was a reluctant acceptance that this was the end of the road for me; the journey had ended. The death watch had begun. Tears were becoming the norm as medical test after medical test began revealing that all of my vital organs; Heart, Lungs and Kidneys were completely dead.

Me and my little boy

Satan had done a great job in presenting the facts to my friends and family. If we had gone by the facts then the casket would have been picked out and the songs to be sung would have already been printed on the funeral program because the facts said ALL HOPE IS GONE.

A person absolutely cannot live without the function of their major organs and each one of mine no longer operated in my body. Perhaps you can survive with the loss of one but not all of them. However, as my small frame lay there and the tubes of a ventilator filled my throat and tape covered my face and as my body bloated to such an unrecognizable state; God had a plan that none of us knew about....He had a plan to show up and show out and THAT'S THE TRUTH.... not the facts!

As the sounds of beeps and tones filled my room my mother never left my side. Death had made his claim and he was determined that I would not miss this appointment with him. All the reports were showing that Karen Kendrick would not live to see the promises of God fulfilled in my life. The mood of sadness was

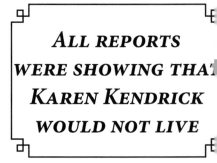

ALL REPORTS WERE SHOWING THAT KAREN KENDRICK WOULD NOT LIVE

overwhelming as preachers from local churches began piling into the hospital room to offer whatever support they could. My parents had just lost everything they owned and the storms continued to blow in these final hours of their daughters life. There was no hope!

In this scene of horror when the news was as bad as it could ever be there was one lady who refused to accept the report of the doctors as final as that report was and backed with medical science. My mother, begin working in the Spirit as only she can and within her a boldness that only comes from a lifelong relationship with God began to come forth. My mother is known by everyone for her earnest prayer life. She began her life of prayer very early in her walk with God and that prayer life has been the salvation of her children and grandchildren. It was on this day in the hospital that my mother began to walk up and down the halls of that death chamber and with the faith of God she began to lift her voice, not caring who heard her and she began to say with divine authority; *"My daughter is not dead, she is NOT dead"*.

Over and over she repeated these words of life; they poured forth from her alabaster box of faith. I am sure that many people; well-meaning Christians heard her say these words and felt sorry for her but Mom had heard something greater than the facts; she had heard that Jesus was a healer and that the saints of God have a right to make a claim on that promise and that's exactly what Mama did; I will forever believe that my healing and my resurrection came as a direct result of her prophetic decree in the Spirit. Her temerity and her tenacity in the wrestling match of faith touched the heart of God and the hand of death was stayed; thank you Mom!

It was soon determined by our local physicians that the local hospital would not be able to provide the level of care that my desperate situation would require of them. So, the family being in such a frenetic frenzy listened to the advice of my aunt Debbie from New York. In her rush to get to Mississippi she was trying to arrange emergency air travel and made the suggestion that I be transferred to *Tulane*

Medical Center. After the calls were made among physicians then it was decided that they were indeed better suited to provide for the care they my situation demanded.

Dad with some of his little
great-grands

ANGELS IN THE ROOM

Chapter Three

They rushed me by ambulance to what everyone expected to be the last resort; the final hope! But God was watching and God was there and God was waiting for His moment to show up and show out; To prove as a lie the suggestion of this world that He is no longer a healer or that He no longer answers prayers.

Everyone was in a somber mood at three o'clock that afternoon when my decaying and decomposing body was loaded onto a gurney. Thankfully even though I had a zero percent chance of living; every effort was still being made at the insistence of my family and friends. *Tulane Medical Center* in New Orleans, La was hurriedly preparing for my arrival, they had been notified of the situation and the hopelessness of my impending death but still as all good nurses and doctors do they were faithful to their oath to protect

EVERYONE KNEW WHAT NO ONE WANTED TO HEAR; I WAS DEAD!

life and they prepared to help me in any way they could. At my arrival I was rushed in for emergency care; the physicians faced an impossible situation; they had nothing to work with. Everyone knew what no one wanted to hear; I was dead!

Specialist from every field of medicine began their official assessments; their gathering of those facts that the world places so much-faith in; those things that defy the truth of Gods Word and scream for and demand our obedient attention. Willingly we surrender to those facts of life rather than believing the Words of God that declare what the truth REALLY is! However, these wonderful and caring physicians are trained in facts and therefore that's all they have to work with. But there is a small group of people in this world who operate on a total different level and I am so glad that I was born into that group of people; I'm so glad they were ANGELS IN MY ROOM.

Many people look for spirit beings called angels when the truth is angels appeared as humans in the Bible many times because in fact sometimes they are humans. Angels are simply messengers of God; they are the ones who bring Gods message into our lives rather than man's facts. At *Tulane Medical Center* there were angels in my room; Mom, Dad, friends and prayer warriors around the world were bringing the Message that JESUS CHRIST CAN STILL RAISE THE DEAD and HE CAN STILL DEFY THE ODDS and HE CAN STILL BRING RESURRECTION POWER TO A DEAD SITUATION.

Angels were calling from around the world; my family was inundated with ministers and people of faith from internet prayer groups who were calling to encourage our faith and it was faith that we needed because the odds were completely against us; ALL HOPE WAS GONE; facts were prevailing and would have continued to do so had it not been for the ANGELS IN MY ROOM.

Then in another dimension walking along beside us in that parallel universe of the Spirit, one of my nurses told us how that she saw that great spiritual host from heaven; the spiritual angels joining forces with my earthly angels. She told her testimony of how immediately upon seeing my dying and putrid body and as they were all rushing to place lines in me that she saw the angels of that other dimension and she testifies of seeing a bright light surround me while she was working. Why were they there? Because we needed a miracle; because prayer was reaching the heart of God and word based faith was moving mountains. What my sweet nurse saw that day was that great team of mountain movers who had arrived from the heavenlies to attack and to destroy the spirit of doubt and disbelief; to pierce the darkness; they had come to alter circumstances and to bring THE TRUTH in spite of the facts.

He was well known at *Tulane Medical Center* because of his unparalleled medical skills; *Dr. Reaganstine*. His professional opinion; his facts were ready to be given as he entered the room where a host of family was waiting and worried.

"Your daughter's absolute greatest chance of survival is 10% to 15% and if somehow she defeated all odds she will be a complete vegetable for the rest of her natural life and ALL OF HER MAJOR organs would

have to be transplanted"......those words and those facts only added to the thunderstorm of fear and doubt that had gathered around my already suffering family; as a registered nurse for over twenty years I am qualified to interpret his words; "*Your daughter IS dead*"

Tulane Medical Center was determined to let me die at peace and give me every ounce of care humanly possible as they began connecting me to my life support ventilator. My body had bloated and dilated beyond recognition and my face was now covered with tubes and tape and all the other trapping of death. My lungs had died completely and could now only function on a ventilator.

Oh how I wish it were in my writing skills to truly convey to you these moments of desperation; the feeling of total helplessness and vulnerability in the air; the tears of the eyes and I wish you could hear right now while reading these words those unspoken whispers of death that were held secretly and quietly in peoples thoughts rather than words as everyone knew that it was impossible for me to live. I pray that God will at this moment transport you to that place in time in your thinking so that you can feel the complete desperation and hopelessness of my life and of my families suffering.

I was dying; no I was dead and my family was dying with me; the darkness was overwhelming and Satan rejoiced as he waited to claim my dead body and to announce to hell the end of my young life. The party had started; all those prophecies over my life and concerning my future would all now be nothing but words if Satan's plan of death prevailed. All that God had said would now become lies in this battle of facts vs. truth! There was a war going on; hell and heaven had met for the great confrontation between Satan's lies and Gods glorious truth......I think you already know how that battle would end!

Dialysis for my kidneys, that's never a good thing! Now, you add this to the breathing machines and the heart pumps and you get a pretty somber picture of facts. In the medical world when the word "*levophed*" is mentioned nothing else needs to be said; it's the code word for "*impossible situation*" or to put it much plainer "DEATH".

My sweet brother, Kevin

I was placed on levophed because my heart was dead. Now, lets add this additional fact to all the others now piling up against me; I was "*yellow as a lemon*" because in addition to my lungs and my heart and my kidneys all being destroyed; my liver is now also dead! The facts were mounting; every organ necessary for life were ALL DEAD!

Everyone was there after hearing of the grim prognosis; the death watch continued. The hospital was so convinced that my life was over that they broke their normal protocol concerning visitors. In my room in the ICU they allowed thirty (30) people at a time in my room to say goodbye and to get their last sights of the living version of me.

What a sight they saw! From what I am told my body was "*blown up*" to the point of not being recognizable. My normal color was now black and blue and my rotting skin completely cold to the touch because the fire of life had left me; I existed only by machines. But, as long as I was there I was NEVER left alone!

Not only were those spiritual visitors from heaven standing guard at my side but so was Mom and hell has never produced a lie bigger than her prayers! She never left me while I was in my coma; faithful to prayer and faithful to caring for my needs and having faith for me while I couldn't have faith; she sat hour after hour and day after day. While hell fought Mom prayed, Dad believed, friends held on to hope; they were all ANGELS IN MY ROOM; all working together to fight hell with the only resource at their disposal; the greatest weapons of all; faith and prayer!

Chapter Four

My brother, Kevin is a mans man! He has been a rock in my life since we were young siblings and this particular day was no different. He is not prone to emotions but is rather very staid and solid and is normally able to hold himself together in order to be a strength for others. But, forever do I hold as a picture in my heart the secret tears that ran down his face while I was in my coma.

I have such few memories of that time when I was uncon-

With one of our faithful church members, Bro. Elmer

Goodbye past and
hello destiny

scious and the ones that I faintly recall are forever cherished. I had only opened my eyes briefly as my whole face was covered with tape and tubes but I do remember at one particular time while at *Tulane* when I opened my eyes and there stood Kevin and from those gorgeous and strong eyes were the tears of sorrow as he was there to basically tell his sister goodbye; I suppose he was mentally preparing for the big moment when he could no longer help me with any human help. This battle was bigger than even his ability to handle; this was in the hands of eternal matters as he stood there helpless.

However, just the sight of those tears of love gave me ethereal joy in my heart at that very moment until he realized I was looking and then it was time for him to step back into his role as *"the brother"*. He immediately dried his eyes and went right back into his customary role in my life; he picked on me! He said with that big Kevin Kendrick smile on his face *"Don't frown sister or your forehead will wrinkle."*

After a lifetime of living with me he was fully aware of my focus on youth, vitality and taking care of myself and my pledge to *"never grow old."* The reason he said this is because of all the tape on my forehead that was holding the tubes in place. When I frowned it caused the *"look"* of wrinkles. He knew from experience that if I had seen those wrinkles it would have been devastating for me (huge smile). Yep, that's my brother always looking out for me!

Try as I might there are so few memories that still come to me from that dark place when I was in a coma; when I was teetering between the love of life and the claims of death. My life was in that twilight zone where life is not being lived and death has not yet taken it's claim. However, there are a few things that strangely I do remember.

My sweet and darling cousin Rachel; somehow and for whatever reason I remember hearing her tell me *"get up K.K and let's go get some coffee"* How sweet she was to be there at my side supporting me and trying to lift my spirits even though she knew I couldn't hear her; but strangely I could.

Also, my cousin Scarlett was so caring and kind and she was worried that I might be cold and she kept telling the nurses to put socks on my feet; knowing that I couldn't speak for myself and knowing how cold natured I am, she spoke for me.

Here is where I must make an honest confession! I can be a bit headstrong a.k.a bullheaded; I get it from my Mom; so therefore it's an honest fault! However, when I felt those cold and slimy hands of death trying to pull me away from my destiny, my son and my family I felt the fight kick in. When I looked at Kent my only child and saw the fear in his eyes and the pain in my parents heart I was determined that this was just not my day to die! I had no physical strength to fight with and I was
bound in this bed; I was David and today I was facing my Goliath. ButI do remember doing the only thing I knew to do; I started and never stopped kicking my left foot. The nurses noticed this continual kicking and they immediately placed protective padded boots on my

feet. Later on they would have no idea that I had kicked so much and fought so hard that I literally knocked the padding off of the boot.

With my kicking I was literally fighting hell and the pull of death with the only part of my body that I could move. That foot represented what was going in in my spirit A FIGHT! I was literally using that foot to say I WILL NOT SURRENDER; I will not die before God says it's time; I will not be pulled into the grave; I was literally dragging my foot and fighting the pull of Satan. I was literally doing as Christ said I would do; I was "*treading on serpents*"!

I WILL NOT DIE UNTIL GOD SAYS IT'S TIME... NOT A MOMENT BEFORE

Today I bear in my body the beautiful scar of this battle against hell because while I was kicking and since the padding was no longer there I literally kicked the bottom out my heel. I had to have surgery to repair that part of my foot where I stood my ground with all that I had. Today, I look at my heel where this surgery was performed and I see that scar as a testimony of my struggle against Satan and his lies when I planted my feet literally in the rock Christ Jesus and pounded my feet against the waves of the oceans of Satans lies and today my physical scars are sacred to me because when I look at them I see the TRUTH; GREATER IS HE THAT IS IN ME THAN HE THAT'S IN THE WORLD!

Even though there was absolutely no medications that could cause my liver, heart, lungs and kidneys to return to life and absolutely zero percent chance for one of them much less all of them to be restored: still people prayed; still they believed and this is the reason that we pray today; because God works through the prayers of His church;

thank God someone prayed for me!

I must take this moment to thank those people around the world who prayed for me and you've remained nameless and faceless; my family thanks you and I thank you. Millions of people still pray and God still listens. Now, the most beautiful words I hear is when someone says "*Im praying for you*" because I of all people know the mysterious power of those words and because of that I now live my life and my ministry praying for anyone and everyone who has need of prayer. I can pray with an authority that many do not know because I am a living witness to the power of prayer. I can pray with authority because I have been there; I have stared death down with the power of prayer behind me. The reason I believe that God has honored me to be so effective in prayer is because there is no room for doubt in my mind that God isn't listening. You see when you've been resurrected from the dead there is a tenacity that is birthed within you and no one can convince you otherwise.

My son; Kent

If someone told me right now that God no longer heals the sick I would simply look at them in pity; they will never convince me otherwise and that fearless faith is what moves mountains. I cannot doubt because I have been brought back to life to tell the world that Jesus saves He delivers and He still heals and since Satan cannot get me to doubt I then pray with faith believing. I not only believe that God exist but I also believe the He is involved in our lives, in my life and yours. Faith is not the same as hope.
Hope has room for doubt but faith destroys all doubt!

Most patients have a single doctor, but with me I had several differ-ent specialist working with me; a different specialist for each major organ that was dead. I was given the absolute best medical care pos-sible and yet they were powerless to help me by their own admission.

I have often wondered why God didn't heal me at *Hancock Medical Center* in my hometown and save my family all the suffering. How-ever, I have learned that God likes to work when nothing else will. Only at the end of the road does God get the credit and that's exactly where God allowed us to walk to; the end of the road; the end of hope; the end of life! But He was there; at the end of our road ready to display His power and to give us a miracle that NO ONE else at Tulane or Hancock could get the credit for.

THE 8TH DAY - RESSURECTION

Chapter Five

D ay after day and hour after hour passed slowly and dreadfully with absolutely no change, the death watch continued. My defeated and lifeless body continued in a vegetative comatose state with no response for a complete seven days *(I do love that number seven)* yet no one gave up! They pressed on; they prayed on and they hoped against all hope for the full seven days!

Nearly just as long as God took to create our wonderful planet is exactly how long he took to create completely new organs in my body because on the 8th day; Gods number of New Beginnings; I was restored to life and for the first time breathing on my own with a set of lungs that were declared officially dead!

The fear gripped me when I realized that I was completely paralyzed; my hands, my feet, my complete body was refusing to obey my commands. There I lay not even knowing what had happened to me but I knew that I had cheated death with the prayers of Gods people. Did Satan really think that I would allow him to cripple me with fear? Did he not know that these fighting prayer warriors wouldn't settle for a halfway healing? As my son Kent fed me and gave me water to drink this was the condition the medical professionals had told my parents that I would be in if I somehow cheated death. But, we do not serve a God of small miracles but rather a *"Right Now God"* who does miracles JUST RIGHT!!! I have learned to not play small with Gods "BIGNESS"!

According to the Word of God *"Out of the mouth of babes"* God would speak and it was when all hope was gone that Kent spoke up and told us all about a dream that he had. In his dream he saw his Mom running around the nurses station. Now, how was this supposed to happen? When he had that dream I was dead and without life except by machinery and now that I had some vestiges of life I had no quality of life; no strength and I was guaranteed to be a vegetable the rest of my life; according to facts.

After my healing I asked to be brought before any other place to the church so I could play the piano in thanksgiving unto the Lord

However, me, my family, friends and prayer warriors held on without every last ounce of faith to TRUTH.

Unaltered by my paralysis I knew that Kent's dream was from the Lord to build our faith. I knew that I would one day run and run faster and then run even faster. Running is one of my passions; before my accident I had ran for ten years always enjoying no less than three miles almost every day and God is so amazingly in tune with our lives that He knew that not running for me would not be living. So, therefore He allowed Kent to dream this dream of me running to remind me that He knew the desires of my heart and what brought me joy and He would not give me my life back without giving me my passions back. When Kent told this dream to the family; they all smiled and they all told him that they believed that indeed I would run again. My baby boy held on to that dream!

The more I walk with God the more I am learning to pay attention to the dreams of the night; not all of them of course, but there is scriptural evidence that God spoke to people for generations in dreams and if He never changes then it is safe to assume that He still does. Sometimes the power of a dream is able to hold you until the reality gets there. I encourage everyone reading this book; just like Kent did, allow your dreams to hold you in faith until you see the dream manifested.

Remember, before creation all of the beauty of earth that we see around us was only a thought or a dream in the mind of Jehovah. All of creation started with a dream and ended with that dream manifesting itself into spoken words and those words created worlds. Nothing has changed today; just like Joseph's position in Egypt as the great ruler, had it not been for him holding the dreams of God in his heart rather than the opinions of people especially his own family then he would have never arrived at the throne. I call on everyone to "*Dream Again*" go back and collect your dreams and if they line up with God's Word and if you're walking in full surrender to Him then expect them to happen; speak them every day and allow your dreams to lay out your destiny rather than your detractors to lay out your demise!

The 8th Day; always Gods number of New Beginnings, was my day of resurrection. No longer living because of machines I was now living because of purpose and prayer and Providence. During the next three weeks not only was I removed from all the machines that kept me alive but now I was even being removed from ALL treatments! As I mentioned earlier the paralysis in my body was a fear that consumed me and as I began physical therapy my upper and lower body began to receive complete healing; feeling began to return to my body as resurrection life began restoring every broken part of me. What an AMAZING God we serve! In spite of what the modern day religious enemies of God will try to convince you of; He has not changed! He can and will do for you whatever you have need of. I am no one special and yet I am alive today because of an absolute unexplainable medical miracle. Believe again! Rise up out of your dead situation today and receive LIFE; declare LIFE and walk in LIFE.

I fought with everything in me to do as my therapist instructed me to do! The walker was humiliating; learning to walk again was so very hard for me but I refused to allow pity to take over my mind; I was alive and I was brought back to life for a purpose and I walked knowing that I was walking into destiny and if I had to start that walk on a walker I would end that walk at the finish line having "*fought a good fight and finishing the course*" for which I was re-born for. Did this mean that Satan was through trying now? Was he now going to leave me alone and let me go running in the calling on my life since he failed in killing my body? It is a nice thought and I confess at times a secret desire of mine but not at all; If he can't destroy your body hell find the next part of you to attack; it is your job to watch for his attacks to recognize them. Satan's attacks are not always full frontal assaults like he did against my body but rather they are usually deceptive thoughts that turn into monsters of the mind.

Satan's only power over you is the power of suggestion; he makes the suggestion and the moment you reject it the battle is over or the moment you believe it the battle gets worse and your mental anguish gets worse and eventually he wins and you lose out by believing his suggestions. There is only one way that his suggestions can be eradicated from your life; listen to Gods suggestions for your life instead! Listen to what Gods Word says about you; your family and your finances; your life.

As you walk in the dreams that God has given you and you believe only what He believes about you then you will find as I have that Satan's subtle attacks on your mind will begin affecting you less and less. Like a little child will he still stand at the fence in the yard of your life and throw spitballs at you. Absolutely! But just as you've mastered the ability to ignore a child's spitballs and you refuse to let them appear as weapons and you give them no attention so you MUST learn to do with the attacks against your mind. Gods says your victorious but Satan says you're a victim. God says you're the apple of His eye but Satan says God has forgotten you. The winner of this battle; God or Satan, will be determined by your choice, whom you choose to believe.

Let me give you a perfect example of this battle. When I first started learning to walk on the walker Satan kept telling me *"You can't do it, you'll never walk again"* and sometimes it seemed as if he was telling the truth but actually he was just telling facts. Yet, it seemed each day that I wouldn't walk again but Satan had one problem; my Mom! She was walking beside me each day and she believed in Kent's dream that not only walking but one day I would be running so therefore we had to get this walking part out of the way real quick so I could start on the running! She held onto the dream, she held onto faith until my faith reached hers and THEN IT HAPPENED!

One day while I was struggling to walk a supernatural flow came through my body; my physical body caught up with my spiritual mind and I stepped into what I term *"A Suddenly of God"*. Through my body began to flow a strength that coursed through my veins; I had touched the hem of HIS garment and right then I knew what the woman in the Bible felt like when *"virtue"* left Jesus' body and flowed into her; I too have touched the hem of that garment with my faith and at this divine moment in time virtue filled my crippled body; Healing came to me in spite of what the modern church teaches; Healing belongs to the believer!

When this tidal wave of golden glory filled my body, forget walking, I felt like RUNNING! Of course mom being the protective mother that she is cautioned me to use a little wisdom but the God we serve when you ask Him to help you walk he goes overboard and helps you RUN and that's EXACTLY what I did at this nurses station; by a faith that's not my own I pushed my walker away and I took off RUNNING.

This so-called vegetative state that man had said I would always be in; that was their identity for me but GOD says I was healed and right now at this moment I RAN and I ran until I ran right into a nurse and as delighted and shocked as she was to see me running she gave me professional caution and forbid my running; being a good patient I did as I was told. However, two weeks after leaving the hospital, I picked back up on running and have done it ever since. I'm not just running for the sake of running but I run against the wind of lies; I run against the wind of worry and I'm running past everything Satan had devised for my life; I completely understand now what Paul meant by *"I've run the race"*.

I knew right then that God was restoring me, without one doubt I knew I was healed and that I would be completely healed! I was walking in resurrection glory!

EVERYTHING NEW

Chapter Six

Do you have any idea how much money the skin care business takes in each year with either false or very limited promises and results? Billions of dollars are spent by the masses wanting to have EVERYTHING NEW.

We want new skin, new features, new hair, new eyes, new nose etc. It totally blew my mind when the God who created me knew just how to recreate me with EVERYTHING NEW. During my death everything died; my organs and my cells and my skin; I was unrecognizable as my body lay decaying. All color had been replaced with nothing but black and blue and yet God had some huge plans unknown to Satan and it involved a complete re-creation!

Tulane Medical Center is so renown and respected; it is in fact a teaching hospital, so anytime a physician came in to see you they normally had an intern with them. In my situation; unlike most patients I had a team of specialist from nearly every field of medicine. I had my own cadre of specialist who would visit me on a daily basis and it was always a grim prognosis; death was in the air normally and everyone could smell it. But after this 8th day miracle the buzz begin to spread down the halls of this medical monument; the impossible had happened and everyone knew it and yet no one could explain it! I was a delight to watch their puzzled faces as they came face to face with a total dichotomy; they faced what their medical training had taught them and now what their eyes were seeing and they just couldn't make those two scenarios go together.

FIRST; THE LIVER SPECIALIST – "*Karen, I honestly don't know to explain this to you*" I listened patiently with smiles in my heart because this doctor was just now catching up with I already knew in the Spirit. I knew I was healed and he was just now finding out. I needed no test to prove it to me because there is a knowing place in faith where evidence and facts matter nothing to you.

When you get the one Word from God you enter into a place of settlement in spite of the facts. He continued to tell me exactly what I already knew "*All of your lab results which determine the status of your liver; they are ALL starting to normalize; it's as if your liver is healing itself*" No, my liver was simply doing what it must do, lining up with the Word of God!

SECOND; THE HEART SPECIALIST – "*Karen we have something interesting to share with you*" I smiled as I listened "*Your heart has abso-*

lutely NO SIGNS of damage and no arrhythmias, your heart is perfect"
You must bear in mind that this is the exact same doctors that previously told my family that my heart was DEAD! When you're walking in resurrection glory then every part of your body must adjust to it.

THIRD; THE LUNG SPECIALIST – *"Karen your lungs show absolutely no sign of damage"* yet this same specialist had said to a host of witnesses that my lungs were completely gone; dead!

FOURTH; THE KIDNEY SPECIALIST – *"Karen your kidney function had somehow returned to complete normalcy"*

My hospital room was more like a fast paced newsroom as interns were writing down what they were seeing and hearing. This went against everything that they were learning at school and they wished for an answer but as the specialist told me; there was no human answer, even my physicians gave all glory to God. I watched these interns as confusion covered their faces with their unasked questions *"How does she have a perfect heart when she just had a dead heart"* or *"Why is there no sign of kidney damage when her kidney was completely dead"* Oh how bad I wanted to tell them *"Don't be confused He's just God like THAT"*

According to the facts taught to them at their school there was absolutely no medicine that could cause life to return to four major organs of the body; I wish that you could have seen the wonder in their eyes as with natural minds they tried to comprehend the supernatural! If you've ever watched the

With some special little friends

TV show Grey's Anatomy then you will be able to imagine what this scene looked like.

A great and wonderful gift was given to me by the Lord as He was healing my body; there was a supernatural exfoliation of my skin. Many people often wonder what skin care regimen I use as they comment on the glow of my skin but I must honestly confess that the credit actually belongs to the Lord because after my resurrection my skin began peeling off of my body from the top of my head to the bottom of my feet. Not just patches or blotches of skin but entire sheets of skin began to peel from my body and this supernatural skin rejuvenation was done by heavenly hands as all my old skin was taken away and replaced with brand new, glowing baby skin.

My entire body peeled several times as God removed all the old and made everything new! Best of all…..the best skin care product in the world; Gods golden glory didn't cost me one dime. What the stars of Hollywood pays thousands for I was given free of charge because God does all things well; He never shortchanges with His work; He's got swag and He goes all the way!!!

While there I was told of the prayers that were going on for me during this time. I still could not comprehend the magnitude in any way of what had happened; what a divine unbelievable miracle that had taken place especially when I consider the reason for it being allowed. This was a huge major interruption by God Himself that had occurred in my life; I had no idea at the time that this was something that would change my life forever and that I would never be the same again!

What happened to me and what was created out of a bad set of circumstances; what was meant for evil and for my total destruction would be turned around by God for my good and for lots of other peoples good; hopefully for your good if you receiving any hope of life from these words then it was also for YOUR good! What good? The effect of healing to so many minds; of renewing their faith in what unlimited power God has and that God can still move any mountain with that faith. It was meant for a purpose of restoration of faith in so many including myself. Actually, it would cause me to have faith I have never known before and I wouldn't have had this life shaking faith if this seemingly bad situation had not been allowed to happen in my life. I would come to know after much prayer and meditation that it wasn't because of something horrible that I had done to deserve such torment as this; but rather I was chosen for this and it was allowed so that I would have a testimony that would bring healing to so many. I feel allot like Job when God told him "*I chose you in the furnace of affliction.*"

Sometimes though, there is no running away from those tormenting questions of the mind when you are forced to ask, Why Me? Why didn't God choose someone else or this? I still can't tell you that answer in its entirety. I may one day come to know its fullness or maybe I never will. However, I can say with absolute certitude as crazy as it may sound; I am so thankful it happened! Why? Because of the supernatural gift of faith in God that I received from it.

I know that this gift however wasn't given to me for me but rather for me to help others in building their faith in God. God loves proving His unlimited power and what He is capable of which is more than any human being can ever be.

Does God love showing up and showing out? Does God love working when nothing else will? Does He love the looks of perplexity among the so-called elite of human minds? Oh, yes he does! He loves reminding us human beings of who really does hold all power and no-one and nothing on this earth is above Him.

Did God do a full and complete miracle in me? Was there any areas of my dead body that was not restored? Surely, I was sent home with lots of medication to keep me alive, right?

I am glad to announce to the world and to all the forces of darkness that since being discharged from that hospital I have never been on any treatment for any of those areas that were lifeless in my body; I give testimony to the fact; I write this book as a living witness and I wish for my testimony to be placed in the trial against the accusatory lies of Satan against God when he says that God no longer heals the sick......Let it be known in the eternal courts of justice that I AM COMPLETELY HEALED by the resurrection power of the Lord Jesus Christ! Every organ was restored brand new and in their fullness of capacity and strength. In addition, after returning home I was able to start back running within two weeks and have run every day ever since as though I never had a pause. God does all things well!

As a result of my healing; a new ministry has been birthed. You now hold in your hands part of that ministry. A new level of spiritual authority that only comes from overcoming the dark trials of life has been granted to me. There has been a supernatural increase in faith that God is using to bring healing to many sick bodies as I begin praying for diseases and dead situations in peoples lives.

I sit back and am amazed at the testimonies of miracles after people hear this story; they are able to believe again and then when I pray for them their faith joins with mine and mountains are moved; miracles are done. If for nothing else, that alone was worth all the pain; that alone was worth a GOD INTERRUPTION

A God Interruption

Chapter Seven

There is only one way that you can convince me that God no longer works miracles and that is to prove to me that God no longer exist and you're a little too late for that! However, many of you reading my story are possibly happy for what has happened in my life but you might not relate because your death is not physical like mine was. However, the death of a marriage, a ministry, your walk with God, your career, your children's struggles or even your sanity are all just as real as the death I endured.

Each of those situations that I mentioned all need a resurrection and God alone can resurrect those dead situations in your life. However, our job is not to convince God but rather to convince ourselves and that is where you and I now have some work to do.

What robs many of us is FEAR! Fear that the promises of God are great but they are for other people and not for us. Fear to claim those promises and stand on them because what if they don't come to pass after we declare them to be? Fear that we will look like fools for our faith. I understand and have had all these fears but I am glad to report to you that I have learned to overcome them and to loose myself from their hold over me and you are going to do the same.

Do you believe for one second that I am any more special to God than you are? Absolutely not! Although I was privileged to grow up in a home of spiritual giants you can believe this one thing; faith is not something that it handed down it is something that is earned and learned. My faith came from my proving God over the years and finding out every time that he cannot lie.

GIVE YOUR MIND PERMISSION TO THINK AWESOME THINGS

Get ready to step into a FEAR FREE LIFE and into the best life you ever dreamed possible. When you take the wall of fear down, then the interference or the hindrance for God getting you to where He wants to take you is removed. I have practiced this: daily writing notes to myself to REMIND MY MIND that *"I am fearless and worry free"*. Understand this: that God takes care of the birds in the air and if He takes care of birds He can and will take care of me because I am more important to God than the birds. My potential for ruling with Him in His soon coming kingdom is far greater than that of birds.

Birds don't worry if they're taken care of or not they just fly around worry free, knowing that they are being taken care of. I force myself daily in this battle of the mind to always remember that I have a heavenly father who takes care of me.

If you are just trusting Him and in the midst of praising Him and thanking Him for taking care of you; He will never let you down! Fear and worry will rob your joy, peace, and happiness. Don't worry about yourself! Here's a key secret I've learned; Get out of "self" and encourage others. Learn to sow and expect a return. Give and it shall be given! Learn to control your thoughts and not let your thoughts control you. Refuse negative thoughts. Give your mind permission to think awesome things. Your problem is really not your problem. It's your attitude about the problem. Put your problem in perspective and get the right attitude so it's not a problem.

FAITH ISN'T ALWAYS FAIR! SOMETIMES IT'S JUST TRUSTING IN GOD AND STANDING ON HIS WORD NO MATTER WHAT.

Proof of having faith is when you are expecting, knowing, and waiting! You have to get a vision; a clear picture in your mind; actually seeing before you physically see it come to pass. If you don't expect and you're questioning or doubting, then you are not at the level you need to be in faith. "See" in your Spirit what you've asked for; "imagine" it in your mind how it will be; and then speak whatever picture the Spirit of God is drawing into your imaginations of the Spirit. Don't lose that photograph in your mind a.k. your vision. To have unlimited faith; believing for the impossible; you have to "think out the box" and "act out the box"and "move out the box" and "speak out the box". Why? Because God lives, moves and operates outside the box.

One prime example biblically was the woman with the issue of blood. That is the kind of faith it takes to move any mountain. She knew with all her heart and didn't doubt. So therefore she was going to get to Jesus no matter what she had to do whether it meant she had to crawl through or climb over. She did get to Jesus and touched only the hem of his garment. It was her faith that moved God, and she was healed.

God doesn't hear your need, but he hears your seed. You cannot get something for nothing. You have to pay the price and sow the seed to receive. Knowledge of this is power and lack of knowledge is destruction. Know that if God did something for you before or took care of a problem for you before he can and will do it again! For example, if you are in pain, God is not moved by your pain but He is moved by your faith in Him to heal your pain. Your crisis is God's opportunity for a miracle.

YOUR CRISIS IS GOD'S OPPORTUNITY FOR A MIRACLE

DOUBT CREATES TRAGEDIES. FAITH CREATES MIRACLES.
The "Bible" is the factory or the store to shop and build your unlimited dynamic faith. Your mind is your logic. Your logic will compete with your faith. Don't place your mind or your old carnal way of thinking as the solution for your faith. YOU HAVE THE OPTION TO LIVE A LIFE OF FAITH OR A LIFE OF FEAR. IT'S YOUR CHOICE TO MAKE.

Only you can put boundaries on your faith. Stand strong and rooted in alignment with God and there's nothing He won't do for you. Get on His page and great things will happen in your life. What does faith actually mean? *"To be persuaded"*. Faith without works is dead. Being "persuaded" is an action needed for faith to work.

Persuaded that God will do it and He can do it. Persuaded that God has no limits as to what He can do and that He has all power to do anything. Persuaded that God's promises are real and that you'll receive. Persuasion is the confidence and hope in something and the expectancy of it. Persuasion is being confident of that the things hoped for will happen. Persuasion it the evidence of things not seen. Persuasion is a product of your spirit man; your heart. Faith perceived as real fact not revealed to you by the senses. Huge estimation gets huge results. Little estimation gets little results.

Perfect the gifts God has given you. Work on them and be the best with those God given gifts that you can be. It takes time for fruit to grow. It takes time for seeds/roots to make fruit. Know this; you have roots through what you have planted and all that you have planted in this Spirit will make your fruit beautiful and bountiful. WHEN YOU ARE WHERE YOU HAVE BEEN ASSIGNED YOU WILL HAVE NO RIVALS according to God. There is no one else like you . Your future is in your difference. The only thing between your future in where God is taking you, is in the "timing" of it; God's timing . God himself is the one who "ordains" you with his "divine ordination" to use the gifts he has given you Remember that your testimony can bring a breakthrough in so many lives. Your hurt becomes your healing and then becomes your testimony.

Music, singing and music ministry have always been a big part of my delightful passions. I have always loved this song: "*Something beautiful...something good...all my confusion He understood. All I had to offer Him was brokenness and strife. But He made something beautiful of my life.*"

Remember that a delay in the breakthrough in your life is not a denial. Also, know that if you allow God to do the work in your life....

He will take what was meant for bad by Satan and turn it around to something good. YOUR HISTORY DOESN'T DEFINE YOUR DESTINY. When you come to know Jesus and give all to him all old things in your life are passed away and everything become new in your life; a fresh start has begun in your life. It doesn't matter what happened to you in your past, God is above your circumstances! You don't have to dwell in your mind in any area of pain in your past. Throw it out and make a new start.

None of us are exempt from storms in our lives, we all go through them; but with the power of faith turn your storm into a stepping stone. Remember in the midst of your storm learn how not to panic. Instead, praise Him. This is a little secret that sounds so insignificant and meaningless but the power of praise in the midst of any situation good or bad changes your atmosphere for the better.

Know that negative will always draw negative toward you and positive will draw positive toward you. We live in a spirit world of good and evil. Good does sense good and darkness senses darkness. Make your words, your thoughts, your actions; magnify the positive. When you start to learn a habit of "auditing" yourself daily you will learn discipline in your atmosphere that you yourself can create. It requires action on your part but you can bring forth such good fruit into your world. Every day of your life that you awaken "expect" good things to happen in that day. Look out for them and make good things happen for others. Look around and decide how you can help someone in their life and watch how good things start to come your way.

Faith; if anyone gets near me for any length of time they will hear about "faith" or will hear the faith in me. The gift of faith I have been given through my testimony is one I cherish and I live to pour into all I can on a daily basis.

I am all about exercising and being as healthy as possible and I'm continuously growing in those areas each day. I have come to learn a "faith exercise" that is guaranteed to build your faith. Just like if you wish to build your bicep muscle you will do target exercises for that specific area. In God's Word He says to ask, believe in Him, and you shall receive. I have something called a "God Box". It is nothing to do with the box itself, in fact mine has enlarged to a drawer. But, it is the act of asking God specifically what you want to receive. I actually write out a "Dear God. ...." note and I am very specific as to my needs or the needs of others I am asking about. I then pray unto God and then fold the note and hold it up saying *"God I have asked, and now I am giving this to you knowing you have heard me, and I am giving it to you and putting my total trust in you that it shall be answered in your timing....not mine. I believe you at your word.....and I have asked and I now show my trust in you by thanking you ahead of time for your answer. "*

I then put that note in my box/drawer. Every couple of weeks I read the notes and the ones answered I put in the *"done"* box/drawer, and the ones not answered yet I put back in the *"to be done"* box/drawer. I have witnessed personally the smallest needs to the largest needs answered. This has not only built my faith up, but countless people that I have shared this with. I suggest it in everyone's life; to give this a try. Faith is something that is to be renewed daily and it does take us being active in building it daily. When we do this, however, it is something that is poured into us....but is to be poured back out to build other's faith in God's unlimited power.

Miracle Tabernacle
235 Old Spanish Trail
Waveland, Ms 39576
www.miracletabernacle.org
Pastor. Frank Kendrick

Exciting New Book soon to be released by; Karen Kaye Kendrick

Secrets from The Secret Place

A DAILY DEVOTIONAL

To Schedule Karen Kendrick for a
Faith encounter at your church or
group or for a book signing please use
the following contact information

P.O. Box 3927
Bay St. Louis, Ms 39521

kendrickkaren@rocketmail.com

www.karenkendrick.org

Blessings from Karen